Rob
from N. M. Howe
27 Sept. 1904

BOOK OF COMMON ORDER

"Juxta laudabilem Ecclesiæ Scotiæ Reformatæ formam et ritum."

Ch. of Scotland, Liturgy

Ευχολογιον

A

BOOK OF COMMON ORDER:

BEING

FORMS OF PRAYER,

AND ADMINISTRATION OF

THE SACRAMENTS, AND OTHER ORDINANCES
OF THE CHURCH;

ISSUED BY

The Church Service Society.

SEVENTH EDITION, CAREFULLY REVISED.

WILLIAM BLACKWOOD AND SONS
EDINBURGH AND LONDON
MDCCCXCVI

All Rights reserved

June 1925
H 51.469

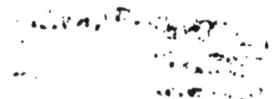

Contents.

PART I.
	PAGE
TABLE OF PSALMS AND LESSONS FOR DIVINE SERVICE ON EVERY LORD'S DAY THROUGHOUT THE YEAR	5
" OF PSALMS AND LESSONS FOR SPECIAL SERVICES	13
" OF PSALMS FOR A MONTH	16
" OF DAILY LESSONS FOR A YEAR	17
THE ORDER OF DIVINE SERVICE—	
FIRST SUNDAY OF THE MONTH	43
SECOND " " "	69
THIRD " " "	97
FOURTH " " "	124
FIFTH " " "	151
ALTERNATIVE ORDER OF SERVICE	176

PART II.
I. THE LITANY	179
II. PRAYERS, INTERCESSIONS, AND THANKSGIVINGS FOR SPECIAL OCCASIONS—	
PRAYERS AND INTERCESSIONS	188
THANKSGIVINGS	209
III. PRAYERS FOR SPECIAL GRACES	213
IV. COLLECTS AND PRAYERS FOR NATURAL AND SACRED SEASONS	231

CONTENTS.

V. ADDITIONAL FORMS OF SERVICE—
- INTRODUCTORY SENTENCES 249
- PRAYERS OF INVOCATION 253
- CONFESSIONS 256
- PRAYERS FOR PARDON AND PEACE 259
- PRAYER OF DEDICATION 261
- SUPPLICATIONS 262
- INTERCESSIONS 266
- THANKSGIVINGS 276
- PRAYERS FOR ILLUMINATION 278
- PRAYERS AFTER SERMON 279
- ASCRIPTIONS OF GLORY 282

PART III.

THE ORDER FOR THE CELEBRATION OF THE LORD'S SUPPER,
OR HOLY COMMUNION 287
- " " FOR THE ADMINISTRATION OF HOLY BAPTISM . 304
- " " FOR THE ADMISSION OF CATECHUMENS . . 313
- " " FOR THE BAPTISM OF ADULTS 320
- " " FOR THE SOLEMNIZATION OF MATRIMONY . 328
- " " FOR THE VISITATION OF THE SICK . . . 338
- " " FOR THE BURIAL OF THE DEAD . . . 353
- " " FOR THE ORDINATION OF MINISTERS . . 377
- " " FOR THE INDUCTION OF AN ORDAINED MINISTER 396
- " " FOR THE ADMISSION OF ELDERS . . . 397
- " " FOR LAYING THE FOUNDATION-STONE OF A CHURCH 403
- " " FOR THE DEDICATION OF A CHURCH . . 408

EXHORTATION BEFORE THE HOLY COMMUNION . . . 415

Book of Common Order.

PART I.

THE LECTIONARY

AND

SERVICES FOR THE FIVE SUNDAYS OF THE MONTH.

Contents.

	PAGE
TABLE OF PSALMS AND LESSONS FOR DIVINE SERVICE ON EVERY LORD'S DAY THROUGHOUT THE YEAR	5
" OF PSALMS AND LESSONS FOR SPECIAL SERVICES	13
" OF PSALMS FOR A MONTH	16
" OF DAILY LESSONS FOR A YEAR	17
THE ORDER OF DIVINE SERVICE—	
FIRST SUNDAY OF THE MONTH	43
SECOND " " "	69
THIRD " " "	97
FOURTH " " "	124
FIFTH " " "	151
ALTERNATIVE ORDER OF SERVICE	176

THE LECTIONARY.

The Lessons for Morning and Evening Service on the Lord's Day form a two-years' course. The First Lesson in the Morning Service is selected from the historical books of the Old Testament, on the principle of conveying an outline of the sacred history; and the First Lesson in the Evening Service is taken from the prophetical writings, the order of the canon being followed throughout. The Second Lesson is taken from the Gospels in the Morning, and from the Epistles in the Evening Service.

The Table for the First Year is to be used in those years of which the number is odd, as 1895-97, &c.; the Table for the Second Year in those of which the number is even, as 1896-98, &c.

When Psalms and Lessons are specified in

the Table of Psalms and Lessons for Special Services, as proper for a special occasion, the Psalms and Lessons of ordinary course are then to be omitted.

According to the Table of Daily Lessons, the Old Testament is read through once, with the exception of certain parts omitted as less suitable, and the New Testament twice, every year.

Table

of

Psalms and Lessons

for

Divine Service

on

Every Lord's Day throughout the Year.

BOOK OF COMMON ORDER.

FIRST YEAR.—MORNING.			
Sundays.	Psalms.	First Lesson.	Second Lesson.
Jan. 1 — 7	i. ii.	Gen. i.	Matt. i. 18 & ii.
" 8 — 14	v. vi.	" ii.	" iii.
" 15 — 21	ix.	" iii.	" iv.
" 22 — 28	xi. xii.	" iv.	" v. 1-20.
" 29 Feb. 4	xv. xvi.	" vi.	" v. 21.
Feb. 5 — 11	xviii. 1-29	" vii.	" vi.
" 12 — 18	xix.	" viii. & ix. 1-19	" vii.
" 19 — 25	xxii.	" xi. 27 & xii.	" viii.
" 26 Mar. 3	xxv.	" xiii.	" ix.
Mar. 4 — 10	xxviii. xxix.	" xiv. & xv. 1-6	" x.
" 11 — 17	xxxii. xxxiii.	" xvii. 1-22	" xi.
" 18 — 24	xxxv.	" xviii. 16 or xix. 12-29	" xii. 1-21.
" 25 — 31	xxxvii.	" xxii. 1-19	" xii. 22.
April 1 — 7	xxxix. xl.	" xxiv. 1-28	" xiii. 1-30.
" 8 — 14	xlii. xliii.	" xxiv. 29.	" xiii. 31.
" 15 — 21	xlv.	" xxvii. 1-40	" xiv.
" 22 — 28	xlvii. xlviii.	" xxvii. 41 & xxviii.	" xv.
" 29 May 5	l.	" xxxii.	" xvi.
May 6 — 12	liii. liiii.	" xxxvii.	" xvii.
" 13 — 19	lvi. lvii.	" xli. 14.	" xviii.
" 20 — 26	lx. lxi.	" xlii. or xliii.	" xix.
" 27 June 2	lxiv. lxv.	" xlv. & xlvi. 1-7	" xx.
June 3 — 9	lxviii.	" xlvii. 27 & xlviii.	" xxi. 1-22.
" 10 — 16	lxx. lxxi.	" xlix.	" xxi. 23.
" 17 — 23	lxxiii.	Ex. ii.	" xxii.
" 24 — 30	lxxv. lxxvi.	" iii.	" xxiii.
July 1 — 7	lxxviii. 1-31	" v. or vii. or x.	" xxiv.
" 8 — 14	lxxix.	" xii. 1-42.	" xxv.
" 15 — 21	lxxxii. lxxxiii.	" xiv.	" xxvi. 1-35.
" 22 — 28	lxxxvi.	" xvi.	" xxvi. 36.
" 29 Aug. 4	lxxxix.	" xvii.	" xxvii. 1-31.
Aug. 5 — 11	xci. xcii.	" xx. 1-21	" xxvii. 32.
" 12 — 18	xcv. xcvi.	" xxiv. & xxv. 1-22.	" xxviii.
" 19 — 25	xcix. c. ci.	" xxvii. or xxviii. 1-41	Mark i.
" 26 Sept. 1	ciii.	" xxx. or xxxii.	" ii.
Sept. 2 — 8	cv.	" xxxiii.	" iii.
" 9 — 15	cvii.	" xl.	" iv.
" 16 — 22	cx. cxi.	Lev. vi. 8	" v.
" 23 — 29	cxiv. cxv.	" vii. 7.	" vi. 1-29.
" 30 Oct. 6	cxviii.	" x. or xvi.	" vi. 30.
Oct. 7 — 13	cxix. 17-40	" xxiii. or xxv. 1-28	" vii.
" 14 — 20	cxix. 57-80	Num. xiii. 17 & xiv. 1-25	" viii.
" 21 — 27	cxix. 97-120	" xvi.	" ix. 1-29.
" 28 Nov. 3	cxix. 137-160	" xvii. & xviii. 1-7	" ix. 30.
Nov. 4 — 10	cxx. cxxi. cxxii.	" xxi.	" x. 1-31.
" 11 — 17	cxxvi. cxxvii.	" xxii.	" x. 32.
" 18 — 24	cxxx. cxxxi.	" xxiii.	" xi.
" 25 Dec. 1	cxxxiv. cxxxv.	" xxiv.	" xii.
Dec. 2 — 8	cxxxvii. cxxxviii.	Deut. iv. 1-31	" xiii.
" 9 — 15	cxl. cxli.	" vi.	" xiv. 1-31.
" 16 — 22	cxliv.	" xxix. & xxx. 15	" xiv. 32.
" 23 — 29	cxlvii.	" xxxii.	" xv.
" 30 — 31	xc. xci.	" xxxiii. & xxxiv.	" xvi.

PSALMS AND LESSONS.

FIRST YEAR.—EVENING.

Sundays.	Psalms.	First Lesson.	Second Lesson.
Jan. 1 — 7	iii. iv.	Prov. i. 20 & ii. 1-9	Acts i.
„ 8 — 14	vii. viii.	„ viii.	„ ii. 1-21.
„ 15 — 21	x.	Eccl. i. 12 & ii. 1-17	„ ii. 22.
„ 22 — 28	xiii. xiv.	„ xi. & xii.	„ iii.
„ 29 Feb. 4	xvii.	Isaiah i. 1-20	„ iv.
Feb. 5 — 11	xviii. 30.	„ ii.	„ v.
„ 12 — 18	xx. xxi.	„ v.	„ vi.
„ 19 — 25	xxiii. xxiv.	„ vi.	„ viii.
„ 26 Mar. 3	xxvi. xxvii.	„ viii. 11 & ix. 1-7.	„ ix. 1-22.
Mar. 4 — 10	xxx. xxxi.	„ xi. & xii.	„ ix. 23.
„ 11 — 17	xxxiv.	„ xiv.	„ x.
„ 18 — 24	xxxvi.	„ xxii.	„ xi.
„ 25 — 31	xxxviii.	„ xxiv. or xxv.	„ xii.
April 1 — 7	xlii.	„ xxviii.	„ xv. or xvi.
„ 8 — 14	xliv.	„ xxix.	„ xvii. or xix.
„ 15 — 21	xlvi.	„ xxxii. or xxxiii.	„ xx. or xxiii.
„ 22 — 28	xlix.	„ xxxv.	„ xxv. 13 & xxvi.
„ 29 May 5	li.	„ xl.	„ xxvii.
May 6 — 12	liv. lv.	„ xli.	„ xxviii.
„ 13 — 19	lviii. lix.	„ xlii.	Rom. i. 1-24.
„ 20 — 26	lxii. lxiii.	„ xliv.	„ iii.
„ 27 June 2	lxvi. lxvii.	„ xlv.	„ iv.
June 3 — 9	lxix.	„ xlix.	„ v.
„ 10 — 16	lxxii.	„ li. 1-16.	„ vi.
„ 17 — 23	lxxiv.	„ lii. 1-12.	„ viii.
„ 24 — 30	lxxvii.	„ lii. 13 & liii.	„ xi.
July 1 — 7	lxxviii. 32.	„ liv.	„ xii.
„ 8 — 14	lxxx. lxxxi.	„ lv.	„ xiii.
„ 15 — 21	lxxxiv. lxxxv.	„ lviii.	„ xiv.
„ 22 — 28	lxxxvii. lxxxviii.	„ lix.	„ xv.
„ 29 Aug. 4	xc.	„ lx.	1 Cor. i.
Aug. 5 — 11	xciii. xciv.	„ lxi. & lxii.	„ ii.
„ 12 — 18	xcvii. xcviii.	„ lxiii. & lxiv.	„ iii.
„ 19 — 25	cii.	„ lxv.	„ v. or vi.
„ 26 Sept. 1	civ.	„ lxvi.	„ viii. or ix.
Sept. 2 — 8	cvi.	Jer. i.	„ x. or xi.
„ 9 — 15	cviii. cix.	„ v. 11	„ xii. & xiii.
„ 16 — 22	cxii. cxiii.	„ vii.	„ xiv.
„ 23 — 29	cxvi. cxvii.	„ viii. 14 & ix.	„ xv. 1-19.
„ 30 Oct. 6	cxix. 1-16.	„ xiii. 1-17.	„ xv. 20.
Oct. 7 — 13	cxix. 41-56.	„ xix. 14 & xx. 1-13	2 Cor. iv.
„ 14 — 20	cxix. 81-96.	„ xxiii. 1-22	„ v.
„ 21 — 27	cxix. 121-136.	„ xxiii. 23.	„ vi. or vii.
„ 28 Nov. 3	cxix. 161-176.	„ xxvi.	„ ix. or xii.
Nov. 4 — 10	cxxiii. cxxiv. cxxv.	„ xxvii. or xxviii.	Gal. iii.
„ 11 — 17	cxxviii. cxxix.	„ xxx.	„ v.
„ 18 — 24	cxxxii. cxxxiii.	„ xxxi. 18	„ vi.
„ 25 Dec. 1	cxxxvi.	„ xxxiii.	Eph. i.
Dec. 2 — 8	cxxxix.	„ xxxv.	„ ii.
„ 9 — 15	cxlii. cxliii.	„ xxxvi.	„ iii.
„ 16 — 22	cxlv. cxlvi.	„ xxxviii.	„ iv.
„ 23 — 29	cxlviii. cxlix. cl.	„ xlii. & xliii. 1-7.	„ v.
„ 30 — 31	ciii.	Lam. ii. 1-19.	„ vi.

BOOK OF COMMON ORDER.

SECOND YEAR.—MORNING.

Sundays.	Psalms.	First Lesson.	Second Lesson.
Jan. 1 — 7	i. ii.	Josh. iii. & iv. 1-14	Luke i. 1-38.
" 8 — 14	v. vi.	" v. 10 & vi. 1-20	" i. 39.
" 15 — 21	ix.	" vii.	" ii.
" 22 — 28	xi. xii.	" xxiv.	" iii. 1-22.
" 29 Feb. 4	xv. xvi.	Judges ii.	" iv.
Feb. 5 — 11	xviii. 1-29	" vi.	" v.
" 12 — 18	xix.	" vii.	" vi.
" 19 — 25	xxii.	" xii. & xiii.	" vii.
" 26 Mar. 3	xxv.	Ruth i.	" viii. 1-25.
Mar. 4 — 10	xxviii. xxix.	1 Sam. iii.	" viii. 26.
" 11 — 17	xxxii. xxxiii.	" iv.	" ix. 1-27.
" 18 — 24	xxxv.	" ix. 15 & x. or xii.	" ix. 28.
" 25 — 31	xxxvii.	" xv. 10 & xvi. 1-13.	" x.
April 1 — 7	xxxix. xl.	" xvii. 12.	" xi. 1-28.
" 8 — 14	xlii. xliii.	" xxvi.	" xi. 29.
" 15 — 21	xlv.	" xxviii.	" xii. 1-34.
" 22 — 28	xlvii. xlviii.	2 Sam. i.	" xii. 35.
" 29 May 5	l.	" vi.	" xiii.
May 6 — 12	lii. liii.	" vii.	" xiv.
" 13 — 19	lvi. lvii.	" xv.	" xv.
" 20 — 26	lx. lxi.	" xvii.	" xvi.
" 27 June 2	lxiv. lxv.	" xviii.	" xvii.
June 3 — 9	lxviii.	" xix. 1-40.	" xviii.
" 10 — 16	lxx. lxxi.	1 Chron. xxix.	" xix.
" 17 — 23	lxxiii.	2 Chron. i. & ii.	" xx.
" 24 — 30	lxxv. lxxvi.	1 Kings vi.	" xxi.
July 1 — 7	lxxviii. 1-31	" viii. 22.	" xxii. 1-38.
" 8 — 14	lxxix.	" xi. 9.	" xxii. 39.
" 15 — 21	lxxxii. lxxxiii.	" xii.	" xxiii.
" 22 — 28	lxxxvi.	" xvii.	" xxiv.
" 29 Aug. 4	lxxxix.	" xviii.	John i.
Aug. 5 — 11	xci. xcii.	" xix.	" ii.
" 12 — 18	xcv. xcvi.	" xxii. 1-40.	" iii.
" 19 — 25	xcix. c. ci.	2 Kings ii. 1-15.	" iv.
" 26 Sept. 1	ciii.	" iv. or v.	" v.
Sept. 2 — 8	cv.	" x.	" vi. 1-21.
" 9 — 15	cvii.	" xiii.	" vi. 22.
" 16 — 22	cx. cxi.	" xvii.	" vii.
" 23 — 29	cxiv. cxv.	" xviii. 37 & xix.	" viii. 1-20.
" 30 Oct. 6	cxviii.	" xx.	" viii. 21.
Oct. 7 — 13	cxix. 17-40	2 Chron. xxxiv. 8.	" ix.
" 14 — 20	cxix. 57-80	" xxxv.	" x.
" 21 — 27	cxix. 97-120	" xxxvi.	" xi.
" 28 Nov. 3	cxix. 137-160	Ezra iii.	" xii.
Nov. 4 — 10	cxx. cxxi. cxxii.	Neh. ii.	" xiii.
" 11 — 17	cxxvi. cxxvii.	" viii.	" xiv.
" 18 — 24	cxxx. cxxxi.	Esth. v. 9, vi. & vii.	" xv.
" 25 Dec. 1	cxxxiv. cxxxv.	Job i. & ii. 1-10	" xvi.
Dec. 2 — 8	cxxxvii. cxxxviii.	" ii. 11 & iii.	" xvii.
" 9 — 15	cxl. cxli.	" ix.	" xviii.
" 16 — 22	cxliv.	" xxviii.	" xix.
" 23 — 29	cxlvii.	" xxxviii.	" xx.
" 30 — 31	xxxi. xxxix.	" xlii.	" xxi.

PSALMS AND LESSONS.

SECOND YEAR.—EVENING.			
Sundays.	Psalms.	First Lesson.	Second Lesson.
Jan. 1 — 7	iii. iv.	Ezek. i. & ii.	Phil. i.
" 8 — 14	vii. viii.	" iii.	" ii.
" 15 — 21	x.	" viii. & ix.	" iii.
" 22 — 28	xiii. xiv.	" x.	" iv.
" 29 Feb. 4	xvii.	" xi.	Col. i.
Feb. 5 — 11	xviii. 30	" xiv.	" ii.
" 12 — 18	xx. xxi.	" xvii.	" iii. & iv.
" 19 — 25	xxiii. xxiv.	" xx. 30	1 Thes. iv.
" 26 Mar. 3	xxvi. xxvii.	" xxiv.	" v.
Mar. 4 — 10	xxx. xxxi.	" xxvi.	2 Thes. ii.
" 11 — 17	xxxiv.	" xxvii.or xxviii.	" iii.
" 18 — 24	xxxvi.	" xxxiii. 1-20	1 Tim. ii. & iii. or iv.
" 25 — 31	xxxviii.	" xxxiv.	" vi.
April 1 — 7	xli.	" xxxvi. 19.	2 Tim. ii. or iii.
" 8 — 14	xliv.	" xxxvii.	Titus ii. or iii.
" 15 — 21	xlvi.	" xxxix. 17.	Philemon.
" 22 — 28	xlix.	" xliii. & xliv.1-4	Heb. i.
" 29 May 5	li.	" xlvii. 1-12	" ii.
May 6 — 12	liv. lv.	Dan. i.	" iii.
" 13 — 19	lviii. lix.	" ii.	" iv.
" 20 — 26	lxii. lxiii.	" iii.	" viii.
" 27 June 2	lxvi. lxvii.	" iv.	" ix.
June 3 — 9	lxix.	" v.	" x.
" 10 — 16	lxxii.	" vi.	" xi.
" 17 — 23	lxxiv.	" vii.	" xii.
" 24 — 30	lxxvii.	" viii.	" xiii.
July 1 — 7	lxxviii. 32	" ix.	James i.
" 8 — 14	lxxx. lxxxi.	" x.	" ii.
" 15 — 21	lxxxiv. lxxxv.	" xi. 36 & xii.	" iii. or iv.
" 22 — 28	lxxxvii. lxxxviii.	Hosea v. 8 & vi. 1-6.	" v.
" 29 Aug. 4	xc.	" x. 12 & xi.	1 Peter i.
Aug. 5 — 11	xciii. xciv.	Joel xiii. 9 & xiv.	" ii.
" 12 — 18	xcvii. xcviii.	Joel ii. 12	" iii.
" 19 — 25	cii.	" iii. 9.	" iv. & v.
" 26 Sept. 1	civ.	Amos v. 1-17.	2 Peter i.
Sept. 2 — 8	cvi.	Obad.	" iii.
" 9 — 15	cviii. cix.	Jonah i. & ii.	1 John i. & ii. 1-6.
" 16 — 22	cxii. cxiii.	Mic. iv. or v.	" iii.
" 23 — 29	cxvi. cxvii.	" vii.	" iv.
" 30 Oct. 6	cxix. 1-16	Nah. i.	" v.
Oct. 7 — 13	cxix. 41-56	Hab. ii. 1-14.	2 John.
" 14 — 20	cxix. 81-96	Zeph. i. or ii.	3 John.
" 21 — 27	cxix. 121-136	Hag. i. & ii. 1-9.	Jude.
" 28 Nov. 3	cxix. 161-176	Zech. i.	Rev. i.
Nov. 4 — 10	cxxiii. cxxiv. cxxv.	" ii.	" ii.
" 11 — 17	cxxviii. cxxix.	" viii. 1-17.	" iii.
" 18 — 24	cxxxii. cxxxiii.	" x.	" iv. & v.
" 25 Dec. 1	cxxxvi.	" xi.	" vi. or vii.
Dec. 2 — 8	cxxxix.	" xii. & xiii.	" xiv.
" 9 — 15	cxlii. cxliii.	" xiv.	" xviii.&xix.1-10.
" 16 — 22	cxlv. cxlvi.	Mal. i.	" xx.
" 23 — 29	cxlviii. cxlix. cl.	" ii.	" xxi.
" 30 — 31	cii.	" iii. & iv.	" xxii.

ALTERNATIVE TABLE.—MORNING.

Sundays.	Psalms.	First Lesson.	Second Lesson.
Jan. 1 — 7	i. ii.	Gen. i.	John i. 1-18.
" 8 — 14	v. vi.	" ii.	Luke i. 26-56.
" 15 — 21	ix.	" iii.	Matt. i.
" 22 — 28	xi. xii.	" vi.	Luke ii. 1-20.
" 29 Feb. 4	xv. xvi.	" vii.	Matt. ii.
Feb. 5 — 11	xviii. 1-29.	" viii.	John i. 19.
" 12 — 18	xix.	" ix. 1-19.	Matt. iii.
" 19 — 25	xxii.	" xii.	John iii. 1-21.
" 26 Mar. 3	xxv.	" xxii.	" iv. 1-26.
Mar. 4 — 10	xxviii. xxix.	" xxviii.	Luke iv. 16-37.
" 11 — 17	xxxii. xxxiii.	" xxxvii. 1-28.	" v. 1-26.
" 18 — 24	xxxv.	" xlii. 1-28.	John v. 19.
" 25 — 31	xxxvii.	" xliii.	Matt. iv.
April 1 — 7	xxxix. xl.	" xlv.	" v. 1-20.
" 8 — 14	xlii. xliii.	" { xlvi. 1-7, 28-34 & xlvii. 1-12 }	" vi. 1-18.
" 15 — 21	xlv.	" xlviii.	" vi. 19.
" 22 — 28	xlvii. xlviii.	" xlix.	" vii.
" 29 May 5	l.	Ex. ii.	" xi.
May 6 — 12	liii. liii.	" iii.	" xii. 1-21.
" 13 — 19	lvi. lvii.	" v.	" xiii. 1-30.
" 20 — 26	lx. lxi.	" xii. 1-36.	" xiii. 31.
" 27 June 2	lxiv. lxv.	" xiv.	" ix. 18.
June 3 — 9	lxviii.	" xv.	" x. 1-20.
" 10 — 16	lxx. lxxi.	" xvi. 1-19.	" xiv. 14.
" 17 — 23	lxxiii.	" xx. 1-23.	John vi. 35-59.
" 24 — 30	lxxv. lxxvi.	Deut. i. 19	Matt. xvi.
July 1 — 7	lxxviii. 1-31.	" iv. 28-40.	" xvii. 1-21.
" 8 — 14	lxxix.	" ix.	" xviii. 1-20.
" 15 — 21	lxxxii. lxxxiii.	" xviii.	Luke x. 1-24.
" 22 — 28	lxxxvi.	" xxxiii.	John vii. 14-31.
" 29 Aug. 4	lxxxix.	Josh. iii.	" vii. 32-52.
Aug. 5 — 11	xci. xcii.	" vii.	Luke x. 25.
" 12 — 18	xcv. xcvi.	" xxiv. 1-25.	" xi. 1-13.
" 19 — 25	xcix. c. ci.	Judges ii.	" xii. 1-21.
" 26 Sept. 1	ciii.	Ruth i.	" xii. 22-48.
Sept. 2 — 8	cv.	1 Sam. iii.	John ix. 1-25.
" 9 — 15	cvii.	" xii.	" x. 1-18.
" 16 — 22	cx. cxi.	" xv. 1-23.	" xi. 19-46.
" 23 — 29	cxiv. cxv.	" xvi. 1-13.	" xii. 12-36.
" 30 Oct. 6	cxviii.	2 Sam. vii.	" xiii.
Oct. 7 — 13	cxix. 17-40.	" xii. 1-23.	" xiv.
" 14 — 20	cxix. 57-80.	1 Kings iii. 1-15.	" xv.
" 21 — 27	cxix. 97-120.	" vi. 11.	" xvi.
" 28 Nov. 3	cxix. 137-160.	" ix. 1-14.	" xvii.
Nov. 4 — 10	cxx. cxxi. cxxii.	" xvii.	" xviii. 1-27.
" 11 — 17	cxxvi. cxxvii.	" xviii. 17.	Luke xxiii. 1-25.
" 18 — 24	cxxx. cxxxi.	" xix.	" xxiii. 26-49.
" 25 Dec. 1	cxxxiv. cxxxv.	2 Kings ii.	John xix. 25.
Dec. 2 — 8	cxxxvii. cxxxviii.	" v. 1-19.	" xx. 1-18.
" 9 — 15	cxl. cxli.	2 Chron. xxxvi. 1-21.	Luke xxiv. 13-35.
" 16 — 22	cxliv.	Neh. viii.	John xx. 19.
" 23 — 29	cxlvii.	Job. i.	" xxi.
" 30 — 31	xc. xci.	" xlii.	Acts i. 1-14.

ALTERNATIVE TABLE.—EVENING.

Sundays.	Psalms.	First Lesson.	Second Lesson.
Jan. 1 — 7	iii. iv.	Isaiah i. 1-20	Acts ii. 1-21.
" 8 — 14	vii. viii.	" ii.	" ii. 22.
" 15 — 21	x.	" v. 1-17.	" vi.
" 22 — 28	xiii. xiv.	" vi.	" ix. 1-22.
" 29 Feb. 4	xvii.	" vii. 10.	" xi. 1-18.
Feb. 5 — 11	xviii. 30.	" ix.	" xvi. 14.
" 12 — 18	xx. xxi.	" xi.	" xxvi.
" 19 — 25	xxiii. xxiv.	" xxv.	Rom. i. 1-25.
" 26 Mar. 3	xxvi. xxvii	" xxvi.	" iv.
Mar. 4 — 10	xxx. xxxi.	" xxxv.	" v.
" 11 — 17	xxxiv.	" xxxviii.	" vi.
" 18 — 24	xxxvi.	" xl.	" vii.
" 25 — 31	xxxviii.	" xli.	" viii.
April 1 — 7	xli.	" xlii.	" xii.
" 8 — 14	xliv.	" xliii.	" xv. 1-13.
" 15 — 21	xlvi.	" xliv.	1 Cor. i. 1-25.
" 22 — 28	xlix.	" xlv.	" ii.
" 29 May 5	li.	" xlviii.	" iii.
May 6 — 12	liv. lv.	" xlix.	" xii.
" 13 — 19	lviii. lix.	" li.	" xiii.
" 20 — 26	lxii. lxiii.	" lii.	" xiv. 1-20.
" 27 June 2	lxvi. lxvii.	" liii.	" xv. 1-20.
June 3 — 9	lxix.	" liv.	" xv. 21.
" 10 — 16	lxxii.	" lv.	2 Cor. iv.
" 17 — 23	lxxiv.	" lviii.	" v.
" 24 — 30	lxxvii.	" lix.	" vi.
July 1 — 7	lxxviii. 32.	" lx.	Gal. iii.
" 8 — 14	lxxx. lxxxi	" lxi.	Eph. i.
" 15 — 21	lxxxiv. lxxxv.	" lxii	" ii.
" 22 — 28	lxxxvii. lxxxviii.	" lxiii.	" iii.
" 29 Aug. 4	xc.	" lxiv.	" iv.
Aug. 5 — 11	xciii. xciv.	" lxv	" v.
" 12 — 18	xcvii. xcviii.	Jer. xiv. 7	Phil. ii. 1-18.
" 19 — 25	cii.	" xvii. 5	Col. iii.
" 26 Sept. 1	civ.	" xxxi. 1-20	1 Thes. v.
Sept. 2 — 8	cvi.	" xxxiii. 1-16.	2 Thes. ii.
" 9 — 15	cviii. cix.	Lam. iii. 22-59.	Heb. i.
" 16 — 22	cxii. cxiii.	Ezek. i.	" ii.
" 23 — 29	cxvi. cxvii.	" x.	" iii.
" 30 Oct. 6	cxix. 1-16.	" xxxiii. 1-20.	" iv.
Oct. 7 — 13	cxix. 41-56	" xxxiv. 11.	" x.
" 14 — 20	cxix. 81-96	" xxxvii. 1-14	" xi.
" 21 — 27	cxix. 121-136	" xliii. 1-12.	" xii.
" 28 Nov. 3	cxix. 161-176	" xlvii. 1-12	James ii.
Nov. 4 — 10	cxxiii. cxxiv. cxxv.	Dan. iii.	1 Peter ii.
" 11 — 17	cxxviii. cxxix.	" vi.	1 John v.
" 18 — 24	cxxxii. cxxxiii.	" ix.	Rev. i.
" 25 Dec. 1	cxxxvi.	Amos. v. 1-15.	" iii.
Dec. 2 — 8	cxxxix.	Mic. v.	" v.
" 9 — 15	cxlii. cxliii.	" vi.	" xix.
" 16 — 22	cxlv. cxlvi.	Hab. iii.	" xx.
" 23 — 29	cxlviii. cxlix. cl.	Zech. xiii.	" xxi.
" 30 — 31	ciii.	Mal. iii.	" xxii.

Table

of

Psalms and Lessons

for

Special Services.

BOOK OF COMMON ORDER.

	Psalms.	First Lesson.	Second Lesson.

Christmas Day.
Morning.. xlv. lxxxv........ Isaiah ix. 1-7...... Luke ii. 1-20.
Evening.. lxxxix. cx. cxxxii. „ xi. & xii.... John i. 1-18 or
                                                                                                                                                                    Heb. i. 1-12.

Good Friday.*
Morning.. xxii. xl.......... Gen. xxii. 1-19, or John xix. 1-37.
                                                                          Lev. xvi.
Evening.. lxix. lxxxviii..... Isaiah liii. 13, & liii. Matt. xxvii. 45, or
                                                                                                                                                                   Heb. x. 1-25.

Easter Sunday.†
Morning.. ii. cx. cxi........ Exod. xii. 1-28 .... John xx.
Evening.. cxiii. cxiv. cxviii. „ xiv......... Luke xxiv. 1-35, or
                                                                                                                                                                                          Rev. i.

Ascension Day.
Morning.. xx. xxi. xlv...... Exod. xxiv....... Acts i. 1-11.
Evening.. viii. xxiv. xlvii... 2 Kings ii.......... Heb. iv.

Whit-Sunday.‡
Morning.. xlviii. lxviii...... Deut. xvi. 1-17, or Acts ii.
                                                                                 Isa. lx.
Evening.. civ. cxlv......... Isaiah lxi.......... „ x. 34, or
                                                                                                                                                                       Eph. iv. 1-16.

* *Preparatory Services.*
1. Morning.. cxxv. cxxvi...... Zech. ix. 9........ Luke xix. 29.
   Evening.. cxxix. cxxx...... „ xi.......... Philip. ii. 1-11.
2. Morning.. cxix. 1-16........ Isaiah lxiii........ Matt. xxi. 18-27.
   Evening.. cxix. 17-40. ...... Lam. i. 1-14...... „ xxii.
3. Morning.. cxix. 41-64....... „ iii. 1-23..... „ xxiii.
   Evening.. cxix. 65-88. ...... „ iii. 24-41.... „ xxiv.
4. Morning.. cxix. 89-104...... „ iii. 42...... „ xxv.
   Evening.. cxix. 105-128. .... Dan. ix. 20...... „ xxvi. 1-16.
5. Morning.. cxix. 129-152..... Exod. xxiv....... „ xxvi. 17.
   Evening.. cxix. 153......... Hosea xiii. 1-14.... John xvii.

† *Preparatory Services.*
Morning.. xxvii. iv. .... Hosea v. 8, & vi. 1-3. Matt. xxvii. 57.
Evening.. xvi. xxx.......... Isaiah xxvi........ Rom. vi. 1-13.

‡ *Preparatory Services.*
Morning.. lxii. lxiii......... 1 Kings xviii. 17-39. John xiv. 15-29.
Evening.. lxxxiv. lxxxv..... Joel ii. 15........ „ xv. 26 &
                                                                                                                                                                        xvi. 1-16.

PSALMS AND LESSONS.

	Psalms.	First Lesson.	Second Lesson.
New Year's Day.			
Morning	xcv. xcvi.	Deut. xi.	Luke xii. 13-48.
Evening	xxiii. xxvii.	1 Chron. xxix. 1-25.	1 Thes. v.
Last Day of Year.			
Morning	xc. ciii.	Deut. viii.	Matt. xxiv. 36.
Evening	xxxix. xci.	Eccl. iii. 1-15.	2 Peter iii.
Thanksgiving for Harvest.			
Morning	c. cxliv. cxlv.	Deut. viii. or xi.	Matt. xiii. 24-43.
Evening	lxv. lxxxv. cxxvi.	" xxvi. 1-11, or xxviii. 1-14.	John vi. 26-40, or 2 Cor. ix. 6
Thanksgiving for Victory & Peace.			
Morning	xlvi. lxvi.	Exod. xv. 1-18.	Rom. xii.
Evening	cxv. cxxiv.	Isa. xl. or Mic. iv.	Rev. xxi.
Preparation for Holy Communion.*	xxiii. xxiv. xxvi.	Exod. xii. 1-28.	Matt. v. 1-16, xxvi.
		" xvi.	" xxvii.
		" xix. 1-13.	Mark xiv. xv.
	xxxiv. xlii. xliii.	Josh. xxiv. 14.	Luke xxii. xxiii.
	lxv. lxxxiv. lxxxix.	Isa. liii. lv. lviii.	John vi. xiii. xiv.
	ciii. cxvi. cxviii.	Mal. iii.	" xv. xvi.
			" xviii. xix.
			1 Cor. x. 1-21, xi. 18.
			Heb. ix. x. xii. 14.
Missionary Services.	ii. xlv. lxxii.	Num. i. 21.	Matt. xxviii.
	lxxx. xcvi. cxxii.	Isa. xlii. 1-17. xlix.	Luke x. 1-20.
		" lx. lxi. lxvi. 5.	John xvii.
		Jer. xxxiii	Rom. x. xi.
		Ezek. xxxvii.	Eph. iii.
		" xxxix	Rev. vii. xiv. xxi.
		Zech. viii. 20, & ix.	" xxii.
Children's Festivals.	viii. xxiii. cxlviii.	1 Sam. iii.	Luke ii. 40.
		Prov. iii. iv	Gal. iii. 23, & iv. 1-7.
		Eccl. xii.	Eph. vi.
			2 Tim. iii.
Meeting of Presbytery, Synod, or General Assembly.	lxviii. lxxxiv.	Isa. lxi.	John x. 1-16, xiii. 1-17.
	cii. cxxii. cxxxiii.	Ezek. iii. 10.	" xxi. 15.
		Mal. ii. 1-7.	Acts xx. 17.
			1 Cor. iii.
			2 Cor. iv. vi.
			2 Tim. i. ii. iv.
			1 Peter iv.
			Rev. ii. iii.

* In this and the following Services the Psalms and Lessons form a general list from which a selection is to be made.

TABLE

OF

PSALMS FOR A MONTH.

Day.	Morning.	Evening.
1	i to v	vi to viii.
2	ix " xi	xii " xiv.
3	xv " xvii	xviii.
4	xix " xxi	xxii " xxiii.
5	xxiv " xxvi	xxvii " xxix.
6	xxx " xxxi	xxxii " xxxiv.
7	xxxv " xxxvi	xxxvii.
8	xxxviii " xl	xli " xliii.
9	xliv " xlvi	xlvii " xlix
10	l " lii	liii " lv.
11	lvi " lviii	lix " lxi.
12	lxii " lxiv	lxv " lxvii.
13	lxviii	lxix " lxx.
14	lxxi to lxxii	lxxiii " lxxiv.
15	lxxv " lxxvii	lxxviii.
16	lxxix " lxxxi	lxxxii " lxxxv.
17	lxxxvi " lxxxviii	lxxxix.
18	xc " xcii	xciii " xciv.
19	xcv " xcvii	xcviii " ci.
20	cii " ciii	civ.
21	cv	cvi.
22	cvii	cviii " cix.
23	cx to cxiii	cxiv " cxv.
24	cxvi " cxviii	cxix 1-32.
25	cxix 33-72	cxix 73-104.
26	cxix 105-144	cxix 145-176.
27	cxx to cxxv	cxxvi to cxxxi.
28	cxxxii " cxxxv	cxxxvi " cxxxviii.
29	cxxxix " cxli	cxlii " cxliii.
30	cxliv " cxlvi	cxlvii " cl.

Table

of

Daily Lessons for a Year.

JANUARY.

	MORNING.	
Day.	First Lesson.	Second Lesson.
1	Genesis i. & ii., 1-3	Matt. i.
2	" iii.	" ii.
3	" v. 1-27	" iii.
4	" vi. 9, & vii. 1-10	" iv. 1-22.
5	" viii. 13, & ix. 1-19	" iv. 23, & v. 1-12.
6	" xi. 27, & xii.	" v. 13-26.
7	" xiv.	" v. 27, & vi. 1-18.
8	" xvi.	" vi. 19.
9	" xviii.	" vii.
10	" xx.	" viii. 1-17.
11	" xxii. 1-19	" viii. 18.
12	" xxiv. 1-28	" ix. 1-17.
13	" xxv.	" ix. 18.
14	" xxvii. 1-40	" x. 1-23.
15	" xxix. 1-20	" x. 24.
16	" xxxi. 36	" xi.
17	" xxxiii.	" xii. 1-21.
18	" xxxvii.	" xii. 22.
19	" xl.	" xiii. 1-23.
20	" xli. 37	" xiii. 24-52.
21	" xliii. 1-24	" xiii. 53, & xiv. 1-12.
22	" xliv. 14	" xiv. 13.
23	" xlvi. 26, & xlvii. 1-12.	" xv. 1-20.
24	" xlvii. 27, & xlviii.	" xv. 21.
25	" l.	" xvi. 1-23.
26	Exodus ii.	" xvi. 24, & xvii. 1-13.
27	" iv. 1-23	" xvii. 14.
28	" vi. 1-13	" xviii. 1-20.
29	" viii. 1-19	" xviii. 21.
30	" ix. 13	" xix.
31	" x. 21, & xi.	" xx. 1-16.

JANUARY.

Day.	First Lesson.	Second Lesson.
	EVENING.	
1	Genesis ii. 4	Acts i.
2	" iv.	" ii. 1-21.
3	" v. 28, & vi. 1-8	" ii. 22.
4	" vii. 11, & viii. 1-12	" iii.
5	" x. & xi. 1-9	" iv. 1-31.
6	" xiii.	" iv. 32, & v. 1-16.
7	" xv.	" v. 17.
8	" xvii. 1-22	" vi.
9	" xix. 12-29	" vii. 1-34.
10	" xxi.	" vii. 35, & viii. 1-4.
11	" xxiii.	" viii. 5-25.
12	" xxiv. 29	" viii. 26.
13	" xxvi.	" ix. 1-22.
14	" xxvii. 41, & xxviii.	" ix. 23.
15	" xxxi. 1-24	" x. 1-24.
16	" xxxii.	" x. 24.
17	" xxxv. 1-20	" xi.
18	" xxxix.	" xii.
19	" xli. 1-36	" xiii. 1-13.
20	" xlii.	" xiii. 14-43.
21	" xliii. 25, & xliv. 1-13.	" xiii. 44, & xiv. 1-7.
22	" xlv. & xlvi. 1-7	" xiv. 8.
23	" xlvii. 13-26	" xv. 1-35.
24	" xlix.	" xv. 36, & xvi. 1-15.
25	Exodus i.	" xvi. 16.
26	" iii.	" xvii. 1-15.
27	" iv. 27, & v.	" xvii. 16.
28	" vi. 28, & vii.	" xviii. 1-23.
29	" viii. 20, & ix. 1-12.	" xviii. 24, & xix. 1-20.
30	" x. 1-20	" xix. 21.
31	" xii. 1-20	" xx. 1-16.

FEBRUARY.

February hath 28 days; but in every Leap-Year 29 days.

	MORNING.	
Day.	First Lesson.	Second Lesson.
1	Exodus xii. 21-42	Matt. xx. 17.
2	,, xiii. 17, & xiv. 1-10	,, xxi. 1-22.
3	,, xv. 1-21	,, xxi. 23.
4	,, xvi. 11	,, xxii. 1-14.
5	,, xviii.	,, xxii. 15-40.
6	,, xx. 1-21	,, xxii. 41, & xxiii. 1-12.
7	,, xxii. 21, & xxiii. 1-9	,, xxiii. 13.
8	,, xxiv.	,, xxiv. 1-28.
9	,, xxv. 23	,, xxiv. 29.
10	,, xxvi. 31, & xxvii.	,, xxv. 1-30.
11	,, xxix. 1-37	,, xxv. 31.
12	,, xxx. 11	,, xxvi. 1-30.
13	,, xxxii. 1-29	,, xxvi. 31-56.
14	,, xxxiv.	,, xxvi. 57.
15	,, xxxv. 30, & xxxvi. 1-7.	,, xxvii. 1-26.
16	,, xl. 1-16	,, xxvii. 27-56.
17	Levit. i.	,, xxvii. 57, & xxviii.
18	,, iii.	Mark i. 1-20.
19	,, v. & vi. 1-7	,, i. 21.
20	,, vii. 1-27	,, ii. 1-22.
21	,, viii. 13	,, ii. 23, & iii. 1-12.
22	,, ix. 22, & x.	,, iii. 13.
23	,, xvi.	,, iv. 1-20.
24	,, xix. 1-18	,, iv. 21-34.
25	,, xxiii. 1-20	,, iv. 35, & v. 1-20.
26	,, xxiv. 1-16	,, v. 21.
27	,, xxv. 18-43	,, vi. 1-13.
28	,, xxvi. 21	,, vi. 14-29.
29	Num. i. 47, & ii. 1-17	,, vi. 30.

FEBRUARY.

Day.	First Lesson.	Second Lesson.
	EVENING.	
1	Exodus xii. 43, & xiii. 1-16.	Acts xx. 17.
2	" xiv. 10	" xxi. 1-16.
3	" xv. 22, & xvi. 1-10	" xxi. 17-36.
4	" xvii.	" xxi. 37, & xxii. 1-29.
5	" xix.	" xxii. 30, & xxiii. 1-11.
6	" xxi. 1-17	" xxiii. 12.
7	" xxiii. 10	" xxiv.
8	" xxv. 1-22	" xxv.
9	" xxvi. 1-30	" xxvi.
10	" xxviii. 1-38	" xxvii. 1-17.
11	" xxix. 38, & xxx. 1-10.	" xxvii. 18.
12	" xxxi.	" xxviii. 1-16.
13	" xxxii. 30, & xxxiii.	" xxviii. 17.
14	" xxxv. 1-29	Rom. i. 1-17.
15	" xxxix. 32	" i. 18.
16	" xl. 17	" ii. 1-16.
17	Levit. ii.	" ii. 17.
18	" iv.	" iii.
19	" vi. 8	" iv.
20	" vii. 28, & viii. 1-12	" v.
21	" ix. 1-21	" vi.
22	" xiv. 1-32	" vii.
23	" xvii. 1-12	" viii. 1-17.
24	" xix. 30, & xx. 1-8	" viii. 18.
25	" xxiii. 21	" ix. 1-18.
26	" xxv. 1-17	" ix. 19.
27	" xxvi. 1-20	" x.
28	" xxvii.	" xi. 1-24.
29	" iii. 1-13	" xi. 25, & xii.

MARCH.

	MORNING.	
Day.	First Lesson.	Second Lesson.
1	Num. iv. 46, & v. 1-10	Mark vii. 1-23.
2	" ix. 15, & x. 1-10	" vii. 24, & viii. 1-9.
3	" xi. 1-23	" viii. 10, & ix. 1.
4	" xii.	" ix. 2-29.
5	" xiv. 1-25	" ix. 30.
6	" xvi. 1-22	" x. 1-31.
7	" xvii. & xviii. 1-27	" x. 32.
8	" xxi.	" xi. 1-26.
9	" xxii. 36, & xxiii.	" xi. 27, & xii. 1-12.
10	" xxv.	" xii. 13-34.
11	" xxxiii. 50, & xxxiv. 1-15.	" xii. 35, & xiii. 1-13.
12	Deut. i. 1-18	" xiii. 14.
13	" ii.	" xiv. 1-26.
14	" iv. 1-24	" xiv. 27-52.
15	" v.	" xiv. 53.
16	" vii.	" xv. 1-41.
17	" ix. & x. 1-10	" xv. 42, & xvi.
18	" xi. 18	Luke i. 1-25.
19	" xiii.	" i. 26-56.
20	" xvi. 1-17	" i. 57.
21	" xviii.	" ii. 1-20.
22	" xxi. 22, & xxii. 1-7	" ii. 21-38.
23	" xxvi.	" ii. 39.
24	" xxviii. 1-14	" iii. 1-22.
25	" xxviii. 47	" iv. 1-30.
26	" xxx.	" iv. 31, & v. 1-11.
27	" xxxii. 1-43	" v. 12.
28	" xxxiv.	" vi. 1-19.
29	Joshua ii.	" vi. 20.
30	" iv.	" vii. 1-23.
31	" vii.	" vii. 24.

MARCH.

EVENING.

Day.	First Lesson.	Second Lesson.
1	Num. vi.	Rom. xiii.
2	" x. 11	" xiv., & xv. 1-7.
3	" xi. 24	" xv. 8.
4	" xiii.	" xvi.
5	" xiv. 26	1 Cor. i. 1-25.
6	" xvi. 23	" i. 26, & ii.
7	" xx.	" iii.
8	" xxii. 1-35	" iv. 1-17.
9	" xxiv.	" iv. 18, & v.
10	" xxvii.	" vi.
11	" xxxv. 9-33	" vii. 1-24.
12	Deut. i. 19	" vii. 25.
13	" iii.	" viii.
14	" iv. 25-40	" ix.
15	" vi.	" x.
16	" viii.	" xi.
17	" x. 11, & xi. 1-17	" xii. 1-27.
18	" xii.	" xii. 28, & xiii.
19	" xiv. 22, & xv. 1-15.	" xiv. 1-19.
20	" xvii. 8	" xiv. 20.
21	" xx.	" xv. 1-34.
22	" xxiv. 8	" xv. 35.
23	" xxvii.	" xvi.
24	" xxviii. 15-46	2 Cor. i.
25	" xxix.	" ii.
26	" xxxi.	" iii.
27	" xxxii. 44, & xxxiii.	" iv.
28	Joshua i.	" v.
29	" iii.	" vi.
30	" v. 13, & vi.	" vii.
31	" viii. 1-29	" viii.

APRIL.

Day.	First Lesson.	Second Lesson.
	MORNING.	
1	Joshua ix.	Luke viii. 1-25.
2	" xiv.	" viii. 26.
3	" xviii. 1-10	" ix. 1-27.
4	" xxii. 11	" ix. 28-50.
5	" xxiv.	" ix. 51, & x. 1-16.
6	Judges iii. 1-11	" x. 17.
7	" v.	" xi. 1-28.
8	" vi. 24	" xi. 29.
9	" viii. 32, & ix. 1-24.	" xii. 1-34.
10	" xi. 1-28	" xii. 35.
11	" xiii.	" xiii. 1-17.
12	" xv.	" xiii. 18.
13	Ruth i.	" xiv. 1-24.
14	" iii.	" xiv. 25, & xv. 1-10.
15	1 Samuel i.	" xv. 11.
16	" ii. 21	" xvi.
17	" iv.	" xvii. 1-19.
18	" vi.	" xvii. 20.
19	" viii.	" xviii. 1-30.
20	" x.	" xviii. 31, & xix. 1-10.
21	" xii.	" xix. 11-27.
22	" xiv. 1-23	" xix. 28.
23	" xv.	" xx. 1-26.
24	" xvii. 1-30	" xx. 27, & xxi. 1-4.
25	" xvii. 55, & xviii. 1-16.	" xxi. 5.
26	" xx. 1-17	" xxii. 1-30.
27	" xxi.	" xxii. 31-53.
28	" xxiii.	" xxii. 54, & xxiii. 1-25.
29	" xxvi.	" xxiii. 26-49.
30	" xxx. 1-25	" xxiii. 50, & xxiv. 1-12.

APRIL.

Day.	First Lesson.	Second Lesson.
	EVENING.	
1	Joshua x. 1-15	2 Cor. ix.
2	" xv. 1-19	" x.
3	" xxi. 43, & xxii. 1-10.	" xi. 1-29.
4	" xxiii.	" xi. 30, & xii. 1-13.
5	Judges ii.	" xii. 14, & xiii.
6	" iv.	Gal. i.
7	" vi. 1-23	" ii.
8	" vii.	" iii.
9	" x.	" iv. 1-20.
10	" xi. 29, & xii. 1-7.	" iv. 21, & v. 1-12.
11	" xiv.	" v. 13.
12	" xvi.	" vi.
13	Ruth ii.	Eph. i. 1-14.
14	" iv.	" i. 15, & ii. 1-10.
15	1 Samuel ii. 1-20	" ii. 11.
16	" iii.	" iii.
17	" v.	" iv. 1-16.
18	" vii.	" iv. 17, & v. 1-14.
19	" ix.	" v. 15, & vi. 1-9.
20	" xi.	" vi. 10.
21	" xiii.	Philip. i.
22	" xiv. 24	" ii.
23	" xvi.	" iii.
24	" xvii. 31-54	" iv.
25	" xix.	Colos. i. 1-20.
26	" xx. 18	" i. 21, & ii. 1-7.
27	" xxii.	" ii. 8.
28	" xxiv. & xxv. 1	" iii. 1-17.
29	" xxviii.	" iii. 18, & iv. 1-6.
30	" xxxi.	" iv. 7.

MAY.

	MORNING.	
Day.	First Lesson.	Second Lesson.
1	2 Samuel i.	Luke xxiv. 13-43.
2	" iv.	" xxiv. 44.
3	" vii.	John i. 1-28.
4	" xi.	" i. 29.
5	" xiv. 1-25	" ii.
6	" xv. 32, & xvi. 1-14	" iii. 1-21.
7	" xvii. 24, & xviii. 1-17.	" iii. 22.
8	" xix. 9-23	" iv. 1-30.
9	" xxi. 1-14	" iv. 31.
10	" xxiv.	" v. 1-23.
11	1 Kings i. 28	" v. 24.
12	" iv. 20	" vi. 1-21.
13	" vi.	" vi. 22-40.
14	" viii. 1-21	" vi. 41.
15	" viii. 54, & ix. 1-9	" vii. 1-24.
16	" xi. 1-25	" vii. 25.
17	" xii. 1-24	" viii. 1-30.
18	" xiii. 11	" viii. 31.
19	" xv. 1-24	" ix. 1-38.
20	" xvi. 8	" ix. 39, & x. 1-21.
21	" xviii. 1-16	" x. 22.
22	" xix.	" xi. 1-46.
23	" xx. 27	" xi. 47, & xii. 1-19.
24	" xxii. 1 40	" xii. 20.
25	2 Kings ii.	" xiii. 1-20.
26	" iv.	" xiii. 21.
27	" vi.	" xiv.
28	" viii. 1-15	" xv.
29	" x. 1-17	" xvi. 1-15.
30	" xii.	" xvi. 16.
31	" xiv.	" xvii.

MAY.

Day.	First Lesson.	Second Lesson.
	EVENING.	
1	2 Samuel iii. 17	1 Thess. i.
2	„ vi.	„ ii.
3	„ ix.	„ iii.
4	„ xii. 1-23	„ iv.
5	„ xv. 1-31	„ v.
6	„ xvi. 15, & xvii. 1-23.	2 Thess. i.
7	„ xviii. 18, & xix. 1-8	„ ii.
8	„ xix. 24	„ iii.
9	„ xxiii. 1-23	1 Tim. i.
10	1 Kings i. 1-27	„ ii.
11	„ iii.	„ iii.
12	„ v.	„ iv.
13	„ vii.	„ v.
14	„ viii. 22-53	„ vi.
15	„ x.	2 Tim. i.
16	„ xi. 26	„ ii.
17	„ xii. 25, & xiii. 1-10	„ iii.
18	„ xiv. 1-20	„ iv.
19	„ xv. 25, & xvi. 1-7	Titus i.
20	„ xvii.	„ ii.
21	„ xviii. 17	„ iii.
22	„ xx. 1-26	Philemon.
23	„ xxi.	Hebrews i.
24	2 Kings i.	„ ii.
25	„ iii.	„ iii.
26	„ v.	„ iv. & v.
27	„ vii.	„ vi.
28	„ ix.	„ vii.
29	„ x. 18	„ viii.
30	„ xiii.	„ ix.
31	„ xvi.	„ x. 1-18.

JUNE.

Day.	First Lesson.	Second Lesson.
	MORNING.	
1	2 Kings xvii. 1-23	John xviii. 1-27.
2	" xviii.	" xviii. 28, & xix. 1-16.
3	" xix. 20	" xix. 17.
4	" xxi.	" xx.
5	" xxiii. 1-23	" xxi.
6	" xxiv. 8, & xxv. 1-7.	Acts i.
7	1 Chron. xiii.	" ii. 1-21.
8	" xvi.	" ii. 22.
9	" xxi.	" iii.
10	" xxviii.	" iv. 1-31.
11	2 Chron. i.	" iv. 32, & v. 1-16.
12	" xiii.	" v. 17.
13	" xv.	" vi.
14	" xvii. 1-13	" vii. 1-34.
15	" xx.	" vii. 35, & viii. 1-4.
16	" xxii.	" viii. 5-25.
17	" xxiv.	" viii. 26.
18	" xxvi. & xxvii.	" ix. 1-22.
19	" xxix. 1-19	" ix. 23.
20	" xxx. & xxxi. 1	" x. 1-23.
21	" xxxii.	" x. 24.
22	" xxxiv.	" xi.
23	" xxxvi.	" xii.
24	Ezra iv.	" xiii. 1-13.
25	" vi.	" xiii. 14-43.
26	" viii. 15	" xiii. 44, & xiv. 1-7.
27	" x. 1-19	" xiv. 8.
28	Neh. ii.	" xv. 1-35.
29	" v.	" xv. 36, & xvi. 1-15.
30	" viii.	" xvi. 16.

JUNE.

Day.	First Lesson.	Second Lesson.
	EVENING.	
1	2 Kings xvii. 24	Hebrews x. 19.
2	" xix. 1-19	" xi. 1-16.
3	" xx.	" xi. 17.
4	" xxii.	" xii.
5	" xxiii. 24, & xxiv. 1-7.	" xiii.
6	" xxv. 8.	James i.
7	1 Chron. xv.	" ii.
8	" xvii.	" iii.
9	" xxii. & xxiii. 1	" iv.
10	" xxix.	" v.
11	2 Chron. xii.	1 Peter i. 1-21.
12	" xiv.	" i. 22, & ii. 1-10.
13	" xvi.	" ii. 11, & iii. 1-7.
14	" xix.	" iii. 8.
15	" xxi.	" iv.
16	" xxiii.	" v.
17	" xxv.	2 Peter i.
18	" xxviii.	" ii.
19	" xxix. 20	" iii.
20	" xxxi. 2	1 John i.
21	" xxxiii.	" ii. 1-14.
22	" xxxv.	" ii. 15.
23	Ezra i. & iii.	" iii. 1-15.
24	" v.	" iii. 16, & iv. 1-6.
25	" vii.	" iv. 7.
26	" ix.	" v.
27	Neh. i.	2 John.
28	" iv.	3 John.
29	" vi. & vii. 1-4	Jude.
30	" ix.	Rev. i.

JULY.

Day.	First Lesson.	Second Lesson.
	MORNING.	
1	Neh. x. 28	Acts xvii. 1-15.
2	" xiii. 15	" xvii. 16.
3	Esther ii. 15, & iii.	" xviii. 1-23.
4	" v. 9, & vi.	" xviii. 24, & xix. 1-20.
5	" viii. 3	" xix. 21.
6	Job i.	" xx. 1-16.
7	" iii.	" xx. 17.
8	" v.	" xxi. 1-16.
9	" vii.	" xxi. 17-36.
10	" ix.	" xxi. 37, & xxii. 1-29.
11	" xi.	" xxii. 30, & xxiii. 1-11.
12	" xiii.	" xxiii. 12.
13	" xv. 1-13, & xvi.	" xxiv.
14	" xviii.	" xxv.
15	" xx.	" xxvi.
16	" xxii.	" xxvii. 1-17.
17	" xxiv.	" xxvii. 18.
18	" xxvii.	" xxviii. 1-16.
19	" xxix.	" xxviii. 17.
20	" xxxi. 13	Rom. i. 1-17.
21	" xxxiii.	" i. 18.
22	" xxxvi.	" ii. 1-16.
23	" xxxix.	" ii. 17.
24	" xli.	" iii.
25	Proverbs i. 1-19	" iv.
26	" ii.	" v.
27	" iv.	" vi.
28	" vi. 1-19	" vii.
29	" viii.	" viii. 1-17.
30	" x.	" viii. 18.
31	" xii.	" ix. 1-18.

JULY.

EVENING.

Day.	First Lesson.	Second Lesson.
1	Neh. xii. 44, & xiii. 1-14.	Rev. ii. 1-17.
2	Esther i.	,, ii. 18, & iii. 1-6.
3	,, iv. & v. 1-8.	,, iii. 7.
4	,, vii. & viii. 1, 2.	,, iv.
5	,, ix. & x.	,, v.
6	Job. ii.	,, vi.
7	,, iv.	,, vii.
8	,, vi.	,, viii.
9	,, viii.	,, ix. 1-11.
10	,, x.	,, ix. 12.
11	,, xii.	,, x.
12	,, xiv.	,, xi.
13	,, xvii.	,, xii.
14	,, xix.	,, xiii.
15	,, xxi.	,, xiv.
16	,, xxiii.	,, xv.
17	,, xxv. & xxvi.	,, xvi.
18	,, xxviii.	,, xvii.
19	,, xxx. 12-26.	,, xviii.
20	,, xxxii.	,, xix. 1-10.
21	,, xxxiv.	,, xix. 11.
22	,, xxxviii.	,, xx.
23	,, xl.	,, xxi. 1-14.
24	,, xlii.	,, xxi. 15.
25	Proverbs i. 20	,, xxii.
26	,, iii.	Matt. i.
27	,, v.	,, ii.
28	,, vii.	,, iii.
29	,, ix.	,, iv. 1-22.
30	,, xi.	,, iv. 23, & v. 1-12.
31	,, xiii.	,, v. 13-26.

AUGUST.

Day.	First Lesson.	Second Lesson.
	MORNING.	
1	Proverbs xiv. 1-17	Rom. ix. 19.
2	,, xv. 1-18	,, x.
3	,, xvi.	,, xi. 1-24.
4	,, xvii. 15	,, xi. 25.
5	,, xix.	,, xii.
6	,, xxi. 1-16	,, xiii.
7	,, xxii. 1-16	,, xiv. & xv. 1-7.
8	,, xxiii. 10	,, xv. 8.
9	,, xxv.	,, xvi.
10	,, xxvii.	1 Cor. i. 1-25.
11	,, xxviii. 14	,, i. 26, & ii.
12	,, xxx. 1-17	,, iii.
13	Eccles. i.	,, iv. 1-17.
14	,, iii.	,, iv. 18, & v.
15	,, v.	,, vi.
16	,, vii.	,, vii. 1-24.
17	,, ix.	,, vii. 25.
18	,, xi.	,, viii.
19	S. of Sol. ii.	,, ix.
20	,, iv. 16, & v. 1-8.	,, x.
21	Isaiah i.	,, xi. 1-16.
22	,, iii.	,, xi. 17.
23	,, v. 1-17	,, xii. 1-27.
24	,, vi.	,, xii. 28, & xiii.
25	,, viii. 1-17	,, xiv. 1-19.
26	,, ix. 8	,, xiv. 20.
27	,, x. 20	,, xv. 1-34.
28	,, xii.	,, xv. 35.
29	,, xiv. 1-23	,, xvi.
30	,, xvii.	2 Cor. i.
31	,, xix. 1-15	,, ii.

AUGUST.

EVENING.

Day.	First Lesson.	Second Lesson.
1	Proverbs xiv. 18	Matt. v. 27, & vi. 1-18.
2	" xv. 19 .	" vi. 19.
3	" xvii. 1-14	" vii.
4	" xviii.	" viii. 1-17.
5	" xx.	" viii. 18.
6	" xxi. 17	" ix. 1-17.
7	" xxii. 17	" ix. 18.
8	" xxiv.	" x. 1-23.
9	" xxvi.	" x. 24.
10	" xxviii. 1-13 .	" xi.
11	" xxix.	" xii. 1-21.
12	" xxxi. 10	" xii. 22.
13	Eccles. ii.	" xiii. 1-23.
14	" iv.	" xiii. 24-52.
15	" vi.	" xiii. 53, & xiv. 1-12.
16	" viii.	" xiv. 13.
17	" x.	" xv. 1-20.
18	" xii.	" xv. 21.
19	S. of Sol. iii.	" xvi. 1-23.
20	" viii.	" xvi. 24, & xvii. 1-13.
21	Isaiah ii.	" xvii. 14.
22	" iv. 2 .	" xviii. 1-20.
23	" v. 18 .	" xviii. 21.
24	" vii. 1-16	" xix.
25	" viii. 18, & ix. 1-7.	" xx. 1-16.
26	" x. 1-19	" xx. 17.
27	" xi.	" xxi. 1-22.
28	" xiii.	" xxi. 23.
29	" xiv. 24	" xxii. 1-14.
30	" xviii.	" xxii. 15-40.
31	" xix. 16	" xxii. 41, & xxiii. 1-12.

SEPTEMBER.

MORNING.

Day.	First Lesson.	Second Lesson.
1	Isaiah xxi. 1-12	2 Cor. iii.
2	" xxii. 15	" iv.
3	" xxiv.	" v.
4	" xxvi.	" vi.
5	" xxviii. 1-13	" vii.
6	" xxix.	" viii.
7	" xxx. 18	" ix.
8	" xxxii.	" x.
9	" xxxiv.	" xi. 1-29.
10	" xxxvi.	" xi. 30, & xii. 1-13.
11	" xxxvii. 21	" xii. 14, & xiii.
12	" xxxix.	Gal. i.
13	" xli. 1-16	" ii.
14	" xlii. 1-17	" iii.
15	" xliii. 8	" iv. 1-20.
16	" xliv. 21, & xlv. 1-8.	" iv. 21, & v. 1-12.
17	" xlvi.	" v. 13.
18	" xlviii.	" vi.
19	" xlix. 13	Eph. i. 1-14.
20	" li.	" i. 15, & ii. 1-10.
21	" lii. 13, & liii.	" ii. 11.
22	" lv.	" iii.
23	" lvii.	" iv. 1-16.
24	" lix.	" iv. 17, & v. 1-14.
25	" lxi.	" v. 15, & vi. 1-9.
26	" lxiii.	" vi. 10.
27	" lxv. 8	Philip. i.
28	" lxvi. 15	" ii.
29	Jeremiah ii. 1-19	" iii.
30	" iv. 5-18	" iv.

SEPTEMBER.

EVENING.

Day.	First Lesson.	Second Lesson.
1	Isaiah xxii. 1-14	Matt. xxiii. 13.
2	" xxiii.	" xxiv. 1-28.
3	" xxv.	" xxiv. 29.
4	" xxvii.	" xxv. 1-30.
5	" xxviii. 14	" xxv. 31.
6	" xxx. 1-17	" xxvi. 1-30.
7	" xxxi.	" xxvi. 31-56.
8	" xxxiii.	" xxvi. 57.
9	" xxxv.	" xxvii. 1-26.
10	" xxxvii. 1-20	" xxvii. 27-56.
11	" xxxviii.	" xxvii. 57, & xxviii.
12	" xl.	Mark i. 1-20.
13	" xli. 17	" i. 21.
14	" xlii. 18, & xliii. 1-7	" ii. 1-22.
15	" xliv. 1-20	" ii. 23, & iii. 1-12.
16	" xlv. 9	" iii. 13.
17	" xlvii.	" iv. 1-20.
18	" xlix. 1-12	" iv. 21-34.
19	" l.	" iv. 35, & v. 1-20.
20	" lii. 1-12	" v. 21.
21	" liv.	" vi. 1-13.
22	" lvi.	" vi. 14-29.
23	" lviii.	" vi. 30.
24	" lx.	" vii. 1-23.
25	" lxii.	" vii. 24, & viii. 1-9.
26	" lxiv. & lxv. 1-7	" viii. 10, & ix. 1.
27	" lxvi. 1-14	" ix. 2-29.
28	Jeremiah i.	" ix. 30.
29	" iii. 12	" x. 1-31.
30	" iv. 21	" x. 32.

OCTOBER.

Day.	First Lesson.	Second Lesson.
	MORNING.	
1	Jeremiah v. 1-18	Colos. i. 1-20.
2	" vi. 1-21	" i. 21, & ii. 1-7.
3	" vii. 17	" ii. 8.
4	" ix.	" iii. 1-17.
5	" x. 17	" iii. 18, & iv. 1-6.
6	" xii.	" iv. 7.
7	" xiv. 7	1 Thess. i.
8	" xvi.	" ii.
9	" xvii. 19	" iii.
10	" xix.	" iv.
11	" xxi.	" v.
12	" xxii. 13	2 Thess. i.
13	" xxiii. 16-32	" ii.
14	" xxv. 1-14	" iii.
15	" xxvi.	1 Tim. i.
16	" xxviii.	" ii.
17	" xxx.	" iii.
18	" xxxi. 15-37	" iv.
19	" xxxii. 26	" v.
20	" xxxiii. 14	" vi.
21	" xxxv.	2 Tim. i.
22	" xxxvi. 14	" ii.
23	" xxxviii. 7	" iii.
24	" xl. & xli. 1-3	" iv.
25	" xliii.	Titus i.
26	" xliv. 15	" ii.
27	" xlvi. 13	" iii.
28	" xlviii. 1-13	Philemon.
29	" l. 1-20	Hebrews i.
30	" li. 1-10	" ii.
31	" li. 27-40	" iii.

OCTOBER.

EVENING.

Day.	First Lesson.	Second Lesson.
1	Jeremiah v. 19	Mark xi. 1-26.
2	" vii. 1-16	" xi. 27, & xii. 1-12.
3	" viii.	" xii. 13-34.
4	" x. 1-16	" xii. 35, & xiii. 1-13.
5	" xi. 1-13	" xiii. 14.
6	" xiii. 8-23	" xiv. 1-26.
7	" xv.	" xiv. 27-52.
8	" xvii. 1-18	" xiv. 53.
9	" xviii. 1-17	" xv. 1-41.
10	" xx. 1-13	" xv. 42, & xvi.
11	" xxii. 1-12	Luke i. 1-25.
12	" xxiii. 1-15	" i. 26-56.
13	" xxiv.	" i. 57.
14	" xxv. 30	" ii. 1-20.
15	" xxvii.	" ii. 21-38.
16	" xxix. 4-19	" ii. 39.
17	" xxxi. 1-14	" iii. 1-22.
18	" xxxii. 1-25	" iv. 1-30.
19	" xxxiii. 1-13	" iv. 31, & v. 1-11.
20	" xxxiv. 8	" v. 12.
21	" xxxvi. 1-13	" vi. 1-19.
22	" xxxvii. & xxxviii. 1-6.	" vi. 20.
23	" xxxix.	" vii. 1-23.
24	" xli. 16, & xlii.	" vii. 24.
25	" xliv. 1-14	" viii. 1-25.
26	" xlv. & xlvi. 1-12	" viii. 26.
27	" xlvii.	" ix. 1-27.
28	" xlix. 20	" ix. 28-50.
29	" l. 21	" ix. 51, & x. 1-16.
30	" li. 11-26	" x. 17.
31	" li. 41-53	" xi. 1-28.

NOVEMBER.

	MORNING.	
Day.	First Lesson.	Second Lesson.
1	Jeremiah li. 54	Hebrews iv. & v.
2	Lam. ii.	,, vi.
3	,, iii. 34	,, vii.
4	Ezekiel i.	,, viii.
5	,, iii. 15	,, ix.
6	,, viii.	,, x. 1-18.
7	,, x.	,, x. 19.
8	,, xii.	,, xi. 1-16.
9	,, xiv.	,, xi. 17.
10	,, xvi. 44	,, xii.
11	,, xviii.	,, xiii.
12	,, xx. 18	James i.
13	,, xxii. 17	,, ii.
14	,, xxvi.	,, iii.
15	,, xxviii.	,, iv.
16	,, xxxii. 1-16	,, v.
17	,, xxxiii. 21	1 Peter i. 1-21.
18	,, xxxvi. 1-15	,, i. 22, & ii. 1-10.
19	,, xxxvii.	,, ii. 11, & iii. 1-7.
20	,, xxxix. 17	,, iii. 8.
21	,, xl. 28	,, iv.
22	,, xlii.	,, v.
23	,, xliv.	2 Peter i.
24	,, xlvi.	,, ii.
25	,, xlviii.	,, iii.
26	Daniel ii. 1-23	1 John i.
27	,, iii.	,, ii. 1-14.
28	,, v.	,, ii. 15.
29	,, vii.	,, iii. 1-15.
30	,, ix.	,, iii. 16, & iv. 1-6.

NOVEMBER.

Day.	First Lesson.	Second Lesson.
	EVENING.	
1	Lam. i. 1-14	Luke xi. 29.
2	,, iii. 1-33	,, xii. 1-34.
3	,, iv. & v.	,, xii. 35.
4	Ezekiel ii. & iii. 1-14	,, xiii. 1-17.
5	,, v. 5	,, xiii. 18.
6	,, ix.	,, xiv. 1-24.
7	,, xi.	,, xiv. 25, & xv. 1-10.
8	,, xiii. 1-16	,, xv. 11.
9	,, xv.	,, xvi.
10	,, xvii.	,, xvii. 1-19.
11	,, xx. 1-17	,, xvii. 20.
12	,, xxi.	,, xviii. 1-30.
13	,, xxiv. 15	,, xviii. 31, & xix. 1-10.
14	,, xxvii.	,, xix. 11-27.
15	,, xxxi.	,, xix. 28.
16	,, xxxiii. 1-20	,, xx. 1-26.
17	,, xxxiv.	,, xx. 27, & xxi. 1-4.
18	,, xxxvi. 16	,, xxi. 5.
19	,, xxxviii. 14	,, xxii. 1-30.
20	,, xl. 1-27	,, xxii. 31-53.
21	,, xli.	,, xxii. 54, & xxiii. 1-25.
22	,, xliii.	,, xxiii. 26-49.
23	,, xlv.	,, xxiii. 50, & xxiv. 1-12.
24	,, xlvii. 1-12	,, xxiv. 13-43.
25	Daniel i.	,, xxiv. 44.
26	,, ii. 24	John i. 1-28.
27	,, iv.	,, i. 29.
28	,, vi.	,, ii.
29	,, viii.	,, iii. 1-21.
30	,, x.	,, iii. 22.

DECEMBER.

Day.	First Lesson.	Second Lesson.
	MORNING.	
1	Daniel xi. 1-34	1 John iv. 7.
2	Hosea ii. 14	" v.
3	" v. 8, & vi. 1-6	2 John.
4	" ix.	3 John.
5	" xi.	Jude.
6	" xiv.	Rev. i.
7	Joel ii. 1-27	" ii. 1-17.
8	Amos i.	" ii. 18, & iii. 1-6.
9	" iv.	" iii. 7.
10	" vi.	" iv.
11	" viii.	" v.
12	Obadiah.	" vi.
13	Jonah iii. & iv.	" vii.
14	Micah ii.	" viii.
15	" iv. 9, & v.	" ix. 1-11.
16	" vii.	" ix. 12.
17	Nahum ii.	" x.
18	Habak. i.	" xi.
19	" iii.	" xii.
20	Zeph. ii. 4	" xiii.
21	Haggai i.	" xiv.
22	" ii. 10	" xv.
23	Zech. i. 18, & ii.	" xvi.
24	" iv.	" xvii.
25	" vi.	" xviii.
26	" viii.	" xix. 1-10.
27	" x.	" xix. 11.
28	" xii.	" xx.
29	" xiv.	" xxi. 1-14.
30	Malachi ii. 1-9	" xxi. 15.
31	" iii. 1-12	" xxii.

DECEMBER.

Day.	First Lesson.	Second Lesson.
	EVENING.	
1	Daniel xi. 35, & xii.	John iv. 1-30.
2	Hosea iii. 4, & iv. 1-12	,, iv. 31.
3	,, vii. 8, & viii.	,, v. 1-23.
4	,, x.	,, v. 24.
5	,, xiii. 1-14	,, vi. 1-21.
6	Joel i.	,, vi. 22-40.
7	,, ii. 28, & iii.	,, vi. 41.
8	Amos ii. & iii. 1-8	,, vii. 1-24.
9	,, v.	,, vii. 25.
10	,, vii.	,, viii. 1-30.
11	,, ix.	,, viii. 31.
12	Jonah i. & ii.	,, ix. 1-38.
13	Micah i. 1-9	,, ix. 39, & x. 1-21.
14	,, iii. & iv. 1-8	,, x. 22.
15	,, vi.	,, xi. 1-46.
16	Nahum i.	,, xi. 47, & xii. 1-19.
17	,, iii.	,, xii. 20.
18	Habak. ii.	,, xiii. 1-20.
19	Zeph. i. & ii. 1-3	,, xiii. 21.
20	,, iii.	,, xiv.
21	Haggai ii. 1-9	,, xv.
22	Zech. i. 1-17	,, xvi. 1-15.
23	,, iii.	,, xvi. 16.
24	,, v.	,, xvii.
25	,, vii.	,, xviii. 1-27.
26	,, ix.	,, xviii. 28.
27	,, xi.	,, xix. 1-24.
28	,, xiii.	,, xix. 25.
29	Malachi i.	,, xx. 1-18.
30	,, ii. 10	,, xx. 19.
31	,, iii. 13, & iv.	,, xxi.

THE ORDER OF DIVINE SERVICE.

First Sunday of the Month.

Morning Service.

The Congregation being assembled, Divine Service may begin with the singing of a Psalm or Hymn; then, the Congregation still standing, the Minister shall say—

OUR help is in the name of the Lord, who made heaven and earth.

O come, let us worship and bow down; let us kneel before the Lord our Maker. For He is our God; and we are the people of His pasture, and the sheep of His hand.

Then, the Congregation kneeling, the Minister shall say—

Let us Pray.

I.

Prayer of Invocation.

ALMIGHTY God, our heavenly Father, who hast made the Church Thy dwelling-place, and chosen it as Thy rest for ever, and hast taught us in Thy Word not to forsake the assembling of ourselves together; regard in Thy mercy, we beseech Thee, us Thy servants, who meet this day in Thy holy place. Manifest Thyself unto us, and bless unto us all Thine ordinances, so that our worship may prepare us both to serve Thee now, and to glorify Thee hereafter in Thine eternal kingdom; through Jesus Christ our Lord. **Amen.**

The Confession.

O Lord our God, eternal and almighty Father, we acknowledge and confess before Thy holy majesty that we are poor sinners; born in corruption and prone to evil; unable of ourselves to do that which is good; transgressing daily, and in many ways, Thy holy commandments, and by Thy just judgment deserving of condemnation and death.

We are deeply grieved, O Lord, for having offended against Thee. We condemn both ourselves and our sins with unfeigned penitence;

we seek refuge in Thy mercy, and humbly entreat Thee to help us in our misery.

Be pleased, O most gracious God, Father of mercies, to have compassion on us, and through Jesus Christ Thy Son to pardon all our sins. Grant unto us also, and increase in us from day to day, the grace of Thy Holy Spirit, that acknowledging and lamenting our iniquities, we may renounce them with our whole heart, and may bring forth the fruits of holiness and righteousness, which are well-pleasing in Thy sight; through Jesus Christ our Lord.
Amen.

For Pardon and Peace.

Blessed be Thy name, O Lord, that, according to the comforting assurance of Thy Word, Thou dost forgive the sins of all who truly repent, who believe in the Lord Jesus Christ, and are resolved to walk in newness of life. Grant, we beseech Thee, to all such here present the full assurance of pardon and reconciliation, and the peace which passeth all understanding; through Jesus Christ our Lord. *Amen.*

Supplications.

Almighty God, who hast redeemed us to Thyself with the precious blood of Thy dear Son; grant that we may live no longer unto ourselves, but unto Him who died for us and rose again.

Direct us always by Thy grace, O merciful God, and lead us continually by Thy Spirit.

Give us good and holy thoughts, pure, gentle, and peaceable dispositions, an entire resignation to Thy will, a perfect love to Thee, and a sincere charity towards all mankind.

Wean our hearts from the vanity of this world, and give us grace to have them always lifted up to heaven where our treasure is; so that watching and praying without ceasing, and living in temperance, righteousness, and piety, we may pass our days in peace, waiting for the glorious return of our Saviour; and that when He shall come to judge the world, we may appear before Thee without confusion, and without fear.

Almighty God, our Father and Preserver, who of Thy goodness hast watched over us during the past night, and brought us to this day, strengthen and guard us by Thy Spirit, we beseech Thee, that we may spend it wholly in Thy service, seeking Thy glory, and the salvation of our fellow-men. And even as Thou sheddest the beams of the sun upon the earth to give light unto our bodies, so do Thou illuminate our souls with the brightness of Thy Spirit, to guide us in the paths of holy obedience.

Here may be introduced any other subject for Supplication.

O God, hear us; reject not the supplications of

Thy servants, but grant us the things we have asked of Thee, and all others which are necessary for us; through Jesus Christ our Lord: in whose prevailing name and words we yet further pray:

The Lord's Prayer.
(To be said by both Minister and Congregation.)

Our Father which art in heaven, Hallowed be Thy name. Thy kingdom come. Thy will be done in earth, as it is in heaven. Give us this day our daily bread. And forgive us our trespasses, as we forgive them that trespass against us. And lead us not into temptation; but deliver us from evil: For Thine is the kingdom, the power, and the glory, for ever and ever. Amen.

Here, and at the end of all the other Prayers, the Congregation say AMEN.

Then likewise shall be said—

O Lord, open Thou our lips:
And our mouth shall show forth Thy praise.

Then shall be said or sung a portion of the Psalter, ending with—

Glory be to the Father, and to the Son, and to the Holy Ghost:

As it was in the beginning, is now, and ever shall be, world without end. Amen.

Then shall be read a Lesson from the Old Testament, before which shall be said—

Hear the word of the Lord as it is written in   , chapter   , at the   verse.

Then shall be sung the Hymn TE DEUM LAUDAMUS *or other Hymn or Psalm, after which shall be read a Lesson from the New Testament, before which shall be said—*

Hear again the word of the Lord as it is written in   , chapter   , at the   verse.

At the end of each Lesson shall be said—

The Lord bless to us the reading of His word, and to His name be glory and praise.   **Amen.**

Then shall be sung the Hymn BENEDICTUS *or other Hymn or Psalm, after which may be sung or said by the Minister and people standing—*

II.

The Apostles' Creed.

I BELIEVE in God the Father Almighty, Maker of heaven and earth:

And in Jesus Christ His only Son our Lord, who was conceived by the Holy Ghost, born of the Virgin Mary, suffered under Pontius Pilate, was crucified, dead, and buried: He descended into hell; the third day He rose again from the dead; He ascended into heaven, and sitteth on the right hand of God the Father Almighty; from thence He shall come to judge the quick and the dead.

I believe in the Holy Ghost; the holy Catholic Church; the communion of saints; the forgiveness of sins; the resurrection of the body; and the life everlasting. **Amen.**

> The Lord be with you:
> *And with thy spirit.*

Then, the Congregation kneeling, the Minister shall say—

Let us Pray.

Intercessions.

O God, who hast taught us to make supplications, prayers, intercessions, and giving of thanks for all men, we humbly beseech Thee to receive these our prayers, which we offer to Thy divine majesty.

Forasmuch as Thou willest that all men should be saved and come to the knowledge of the truth, grant that such as are still strangers to the knowledge of Thee, and sunk in the darkness of ignorance and error, may be illuminated by the light of Thy Gospel, and led into the way of salvation.

Almighty God, King of saints, who hast chosen Zion for Thy habitation and Thy rest for ever; we beseech Thee on behalf of the Catholic Church, that it may please Thee to protect it everywhere, and to increase and sanctify it more and more; to remove the errors, scandals, and divisions which desolate it, and to reunite all Christians in the bonds of truth, piety, and peace.

We commend to Thee this parish, beseeching Thee to bless all that dwell therein, and to cause all Christian graces to flourish among us.

We pray Thee for all whom Thou hast appointed pastors and ministers in Thy Church. Endue them with Thy Spirit, that they may fulfil their ministry with fidelity and zeal, and labour effectually for the conversion and salvation of souls.

Send forth faithful labourers into Thy harvest; and give Thy grace to those who are preparing to serve Thee in the holy ministry; pour down the healthful influences of Thy Spirit upon all universities and schools of learning, and cause to reign in them that fear of Thee which is the beginning of wisdom. **Amen.**

We entreat Thee to bless all princes and governors, and to grant them the daily increase of Thy good Spirit, that, with true faith acknowledging Thy Son, our Saviour, to be King of kings and Lord of lords, they may exalt

Thy rule in their dominions, and so govern their subjects that Thy people everywhere, being kept in peace and quietness, may serve Thee in all godliness and honesty.

Especially we beseech Thee to bless her most sacred Majesty Queen Victoria, and to give her grace so to execute her office that religion may be maintained, manners reformed, and sin punished, according to Thy Word.

Cause Thy blessing to rest also upon Albert Edward Prince of Wales, the Princess of Wales, and all the members of the Royal Family.

Grant a spirit of wisdom and of the fear of the Lord to the Queen's counsellors, to the nobles, rulers, and judges of the realm [and to the High Court of Parliament at this time assembled] [and to the magistrates of this town]; preside in their councils, and so direct all their deliberations that they may promote Thy glory and the public good.

We pray for the prosperity of the Empire and all its dependencies; for favourable weather, plenteous harvests, and peaceful times; for a blessing on our fleets and armies, our trade and commerce, and every useful and honest calling. Amen.

God of all comfort, we commend to Thy mercy all those whom Thou art pleased to visit with any cross or tribulation; the nations whom Thou dost afflict with famine, pestilence, or war;

those of our brethren who suffer persecution for the sake of the Gospel; all such as are in danger by sea or land, and all persons oppressed with poverty, sickness, or any other distress of body or sorrow of mind. We pray particularly for the sick and afflicted members of this church, and for those who desire to be remembered in our prayers [and for any such known to ourselves, whom we name in our hearts before Thee]. May it please Thee to show them Thy fatherly kindness, and to deliver them out of all their troubles; above all, grant them the consolations of which they have need; dispose them to patience and resignation, and cause their afflictions to promote the salvation of their souls.

O Lord most High, we give Thee thanks for all Thy faithful servants, who, having witnessed in their lives a good confession, have left the light of their example to shine before Thy people on earth. Mercifully grant that by Thy fatherly blessing we may be enabled to follow them in all virtuous and godly living, and that hereafter we may be united with them in Thy heavenly kingdom; through Jesus Christ our Lord. **Amen.**

Then a Psalm or Hymn is sung, or, when convenient, the Anthem.

Then, the Congregation kneeling, the Minister shall say—

Let us Pray.

III.

The Thanksgiving.

O GIVE thanks unto the Lord, for He is good:
For His mercy endureth for ever.

O God, whose glory is great in all the Churches, and the praises of whose name resound in the assemblies of Thy saints, we, Thy servants, humble ourselves before Thee: we worship Thine infinite majesty; we celebrate Thy wisdom, power, and goodness, that shine forth in the works of creation and redemption, through Jesus Christ our Lord. We bless Thee for all temporal and spiritual good that we continually receive at Thy bountiful hands; but more especially, with all Thy people assembled this day, we praise Thee that Thou didst send into the world Thy Son to save us; and having delivered Him for our offences, didst raise Him up again for our justification, and through His glorious resurrection hast given us the blessed hope of everlasting life.

Here may be introduced any other subject for Thanksgiving.

O Lord, let these our thanksgivings come up with acceptance before Thy throne. Make us worthy to have part in the resurrection of the just, and the glory of the kingdom of heaven, whither Jesus the Forerunner is for us entered; where now He lives and reigns, and is worshipped and glorified with Thee and the Holy Ghost, God blessed for ever. **Amen.**

Then followeth the Prayer for Illumination, in these words, or at the discretion of the Minister.

For Illumination.

Most gracious God, in whom alone dwelleth all fulness of light and wisdom; illuminate our minds, we beseech Thee, by Thy Holy Spirit, in the true understanding of Thy Word. Give us grace to receive it with reverence, humility, and faith unfeigned. Grant that it may lead us to put our whole trust in Thee alone, and so faithfully to serve Thee, that by our godly lives we may edify our brethren and glorify Thy holy name; through Jesus Christ our Lord. **Amen.**

Then may be sung a Psalm or Hymn.

A Sermon is then preached, concluding with an Ascription of Praise; after which the Minister shall say—

Let us Pray.

IV.

Prayer after Sermon.

WE thank Thee, O Lord, that we have now been permitted to hear and meditate on Thy holy Word; and we beseech Thee that its lessons may be fixed in our memories, and impressed upon our hearts, and that they may bring forth in our lives the peaceable fruits of righteousness to the glory of Thy holy name; through Jesus Christ our Lord. **Amen.**

Here may be introduced any special Prayers, as occasion may require.

Then the Offering is collected; a Psalm or Hymn is sung; and the Minister closes the service by pronouncing one or other of these Benedictions—

The grace of our Lord Jesus Christ, and the love of God, and the communion of the Holy Ghost, be with you all. **Amen.**

Or—

The peace of God, which passeth all understanding, keep your hearts and minds in the knowledge and love of God, and of His Son Jesus Christ, our Lord; and the blessing of God Almighty, the Father, the Son, and the Holy Ghost, be amongst you, and remain with you always. **Amen.**

Evening Service.

The Congregation being assembled, Divine Service may begin with the singing of a Psalm or Hymn; then, the Congregation still standing, the Minister shall say—

THE Lord is nigh unto all them that call upon Him, to all that call upon Him in truth. He will fulfil the desire of them that fear Him; He also will hear their cry, and will save them.

This is the confidence that we have in Him, that if we ask anything according to His will, He heareth us.

Having these promises, let us draw near to the throne of grace with true hearts, in full assurance of faith.

Then, the Congregation kneeling, the Minister shall say—

Let us Pray.

I.

Prayer of Invocation.

O LORD our God, we lift up our eyes unto the hills from whence cometh our help. Thou only art the Fountain of life and peace, and in Thy presence is fulness of joy. Father in heaven, from whom cometh down every good and perfect gift, grant us Thy blessing, and incline Thine ear unto us, as we come before Thee in the solemn service of Thy house. Merciful Saviour, who sittest at the right hand of the Father, and makest intercession for us, fulfil now Thy promise: Where two or three are gathered together in My name, there am I in the midst of them. O Holy Ghost, the Comforter, help our infirmities, and enable us to worship in the beauty of holiness; through Christ our Lord. **Amen.**

The Confession.

O God, who hast taught us in Thy holy Word that if we say we have no sin we deceive ourselves, and the truth is not in us; but that if we confess our sins, Thou art faithful and just to forgive us our sins, and to cleanse us from all unrighteousness; receive, we beseech Thee, our humble confessions.

Almighty and most merciful God, our heavenly Father, we cast ourselves down before Thee, under a deep sense of our unworthiness and guilt. We have grievously sinned against Thee in thought, word, and deed; we have come short of Thy glory; we have broken Thy commandments, and turned aside every one of us from the way of life, and in us there is no soundness nor health.

Yet now, O most merciful Father, hear us when we call upon Thee with penitent hearts, and for the sake of Thy Son Jesus Christ have mercy upon us. Pardon our sins, and grant us Thy peace. Take away our guilt. Purify us by the inspiration of Thy Holy Spirit from all inward uncleanness, and make us able and willing to serve Thee in newness of life, to the glory of Thy holy name; through Jesus Christ our Lord.
Amen.

For Pardon and Peace.

We bless Thee, O God, for the comforting assurance of Thy grace to all who repent and believe: As I live, saith the Lord God, I have no pleasure in the death of the wicked, but that he turn from his way and live. God so loved the world that He gave His only begotten Son, that whosoever believeth in Him should not perish, but have everlasting life.

Grant, therefore, that as many here present as truly repent of their sins, and believe in the Lord Jesus Christ with full purpose of new obedience, may now receive with perfect faith the declaration made by the authority and in the name of Christ, that their sins are forgiven in heaven, according to His promise in the Gospel, through Jesus Christ our Saviour. Amen.

Supplications.

O God, who hast taught us in Thy holy Word to be careful for nothing, but in everything, by prayer and supplication with thanksgiving, to make known our requests unto Thee, give ear unto our prayer, and attend to the voice of our supplication.

God of all power and glory, who hast not appointed us unto wrath, but to obtain salvation by our Lord Jesus Christ, perfect and fulfil in us, we beseech Thee, the work of Thy redeeming mercy. Sanctify us in body, soul, and spirit, and guide us evermore in the way of peace. Help us to overcome the world. Beat down Satan under our feet. Give us courage to confess Christ always, and patience to endure in His service to the end; that, having finished our course with joy, we may rest in hope, and finally attain to the resurrection of the just; through our Saviour Jesus Christ. **Amen.**

O God, by whom the meek are guided in judgment, and light riseth up in darkness for the godly; grant us, in all our doubts and uncertainties, the grace to ask what Thou wouldst have us to do; that the Spirit of Wisdom may save us from all false choices, and that in Thy light we may see light, and in Thy straight path may not stumble; through Jesus Christ our Lord. **Amen.**

Here may be introduced any other subject for Supplication.

Give ear, O Lord, unto our prayer. Keep us now and always in Thy faith and fear; and so cleanse our conscience, we beseech Thee, by the daily visitation of Thy grace, that when Thy Son our Lord shall come, He may find us fit for His appearing, and ready to meet Him in the company of all His saints. These our prayers we present before Thee through Jesus Christ, in whose name and words we pray:

The Lord's Prayer.

(To be said by both Minister and Congregation.)

Our Father which art in heaven, Hallowed be Thy name. Thy kingdom come. Thy will be done in earth, as it is in heaven. Give us this day our daily bread. And forgive us our trespasses, as we forgive them that trespass against us. And lead us not into temptation; but deliver us from evil: For Thine is the kingdom, the power, and the glory, for ever and ever. **Amen.**

Here, and at the end of all the other Prayers, the Congregation say AMEN.

Then likewise shall be said—

Praise ye the Lord:
The Lord's name be praised.

Then shall be said or sung a portion of the Psalter, ending with—

Glory be to the Father, and to the Son, and to the Holy Ghost:

As it was in the beginning, is now, and ever shall be, world without end. **Amen.**

Then shall be read a Lesson from the Old Testament, before which shall be said—

Hear the word of the Lord as it is written in   , chapter   , at the   verse.

Then shall be sung the Hymn MAGNIFICAT *or other Hymn or Psalm, after which shall be read a Lesson from the New Testament, before which shall be said—*

Hear again the word of the Lord as it is written in   , chapter   , at the   verse.

At the end of each Lesson shall be said—

The Lord bless to us the reading of His word, and to His name be glory and praise. **Amen.**

Then shall be sung the Hymn NUNC DIMITTIS *or other Hymn or Psalm, after which may be sung or said by the Minister and people standing—*

II.

The Apostles' Creed.

I BELIEVE in God the Father Almighty, Maker of heaven and earth:

And in Jesus Christ His only Son our Lord, who was conceived by the Holy Ghost, born of the Virgin Mary, suffered under Pontius Pilate, was crucified, dead, and buried: He descended into hell; the third day He rose again from the dead; He ascended into heaven, and sitteth on the right hand of God the Father Almighty; from thence He shall come to judge the quick and the dead.

I believe in the Holy Ghost; the holy Catholic Church; the communion of saints; the forgiveness of sin; the resurrection of the body; and the life everlasting. **Amen.**

> The Lord be with you:
> *And with thy spirit.*

Then, the Congregation kneeling, the Minister shall say—

Let us Pray.

Intercessions.

O God, who hast taught us, by Thy holy apostle, that we should make supplications, prayers, intercessions, and giving of thanks for all men, mercifully hear the petitions which we offer to Thee on their behalf.

O Thou God and Father of our Lord Jesus Christ, whom Thou hast exalted to be Head over all, cause Thy blessing, we beseech Thee, to rest upon the Church, which He has purchased with His most precious blood. Illuminate her ministers with true knowledge, and understanding of Thy Word. Send down the healthful dew of Thy grace upon all her congregations. Deliver her from false doctrine, heresy, and schism; and clothe her with the beauty of holiness and peace. Reveal Thy glory among all nations; and bring in speedily the full victory of Thine everlasting kingdom; through Jesus Christ our Lord. **Amen.**

Almighty God, King of kings and Lord of lords, from whom proceedeth all power and dominion in heaven and on earth, most heartily we beseech Thee to look with favour upon her most sacred Majesty Queen Victoria, Albert Edward Prince of Wales, the Princess of Wales, and all the members of the Royal Family.

Imbue all in authority with the spirit of wisdom, goodness, and truth, and so rule their hearts and bless their endeavours, that law and order, justice and peace, may everywhere prevail.

Preserve us from public calamities; from

pestilence and famine; from war, privy conspiracy, and rebellion; and from all national sins and corruptions. Make us strong and great in the fear of God, and in the love of righteousness; so that, being blessed of Thee, we may become a blessing to all nations, to the praise of the glory of Thy grace; through Jesus Christ our Lord. **Amen.**

O God, the Creator and Preserver of all mankind, we implore Thy mercy in behalf of all sorts and conditions of men, that it may please Thee to visit them with Thy most compassionate help, according to their manifold necessities and wants. Especially we beseech Thee to show pity upon all widows and orphans, upon all prisoners and captives, upon all sick and dying persons, upon all who are desolate and afflicted, and upon all who are persecuted for righteousness' sake [and upon any such known to ourselves, whom we name in our hearts before Thee]. Enable them to look unto Thee, O most merciful Father, and to call upon Thy name, that they may find Thee a present Saviour in their affliction and distress; and let it please Thee to deliver them, and raise them up in due time, giving them patience under all their sufferings, the rich comfort of Thy grace here below, and eternal rest with Thee in heaven; through our Lord Jesus Christ. **Amen.**

Blessed Lord, with whom do rest the souls of Thy departed saints, and who hast said unto us by Thy Spirit: Blessed are the dead which die in the Lord; enable us to be followers of them, as they were followers of Christ; and so to run our race with patience, and to fight the good fight of faith, that, our course being finished and our warfare accomplished, we may join the innumerable company of Thy redeemed. **Amen.**

Then a Psalm or Hymn is sung, or, when convenient, the Anthem.

Then, the Congregation kneeling, the Minister shall say—

Let us Pray.

III.

The Thanksgiving.

WE will bless the Lord at all times:
His praise shall continually be in our mouth.

O God, Giver of all good, and Fountain of all mercies, in whom are the springs of our life; all glory, thanks, and praise be unto Thee for Thine unfailing goodness; for Thy faithfulness which is from one generation to another; for Thy mercies which are new every morning, fresh every moment, and more than we can number;

for seed-time and harvest, and summer and winter, and nights and days throughout the year; for food, and raiment, and shelter; for health and reason; for childhood and age, and youth and manhood; for Thy fatherly hand ever upon us in sickness and in health, in joy and in sorrow, in life and in death; for friends, kindred, and benefactors; for home and country; for Thy Church and for Thy Gospel.

Here may be introduced any other subject for Thanksgiving.

Yea, Lord, for that there is nothing for which we may not bless and thank Thee, therefore do we pay our vows now in the presence of all Thy people, humbly beseeching Thee to accept this our service, which we offer in the name and through the infinite merits of Thy Son Jesus Christ, our Lord. 𝔄𝔪𝔢𝔫.

Then followeth the Prayer for Illumination, in these words, or at the discretion of the Minister.

For Illumination.

Cause Thy Church to arise and shine, O Lord, and let her ministers be clothed with righteousness and salvation; that Thy word may not return unto Thee void, but have free course and be glorified; prospering in the thing whereunto Thou hast sent it, and prevailing mightily to turn men from darkness to light, and from the power of Satan unto God, that they may receive the forgiveness of sins, and inheritance among them which are sanctified, by faith that is in Christ; to whom, with Thee and the Holy Ghost, be honour and glory, world without end. **Amen.**

Then may be sung a Psalm or Hymn.

A Sermon is then preached, concluding with an Ascription of Praise; after which the Minister shall say—

Let us Pray.

IV.

Prayer after Sermon.

O GOD, who didst teach the hearts of Thy faithful people, by sending to them the light of Thy Holy Spirit, grant us, by the same Spirit, to have a right understanding of Thy saving truth. Visit, we pray Thee, this congregation with Thy love and favour; and enlighten our minds more and more with the light of the everlasting Gospel; through Jesus Christ our Lord.

Here may be introduced any special Prayers, as occasion may require.

O Lord God, our life, the light of the faithful, the strength of those who labour, and the repose of the blessed dead; grant us a peaceful night, free from all disturbance; that, after an interval of quiet sleep, we may by Thy bounty, at the return of light, be endued with activity by the Holy Spirit, and enabled in security to render thanks to Thee; through Jesus Christ our Lord. **Amen.**

Then the Offering is collected; a Psalm or Hymn is sung; and the Minister closes the service by pronouncing one or other of these Benedictions—

The grace of our Lord Jesus Christ, and the love of God, and the communion of the Holy Ghost, be with you all. **Amen.**

Or—

The peace of God, which passeth all understanding, keep your hearts and minds in the knowledge and love of God, and of His Son Jesus Christ, our Lord; and the blessing of God Almighty, the Father, the Son, and the Holy Ghost, be amongst you, and remain with you always. **Amen.**

Evening Service.

The Congregation being assembled, Divine Service may begin with the singing of a Psalm or Hymn; then, the Congregation still standing, the Minister shall say—

THE hour cometh, and now is, when the true worshippers shall worship the Father in spirit and in truth; for the Father seeketh such to worship Him. God is a Spirit; and they that worship Him must worship Him in spirit and in truth.

O worship the Lord in the beauty of holiness: fear before Him all the earth.

Then, the Congregation kneeling, the Minister shall say—

Let us Pray.

I.

Prayer of Invocation.

O GOD, Light of the hearts that see Thee, and Life of the souls that love Thee, and Strength of the thoughts that seek Thee; from whom to be turned away is to fall, to whom to be turned is to rise, and in whom to abide is to stand fast

I.

Prayer of Invocation.

O LORD God, merciful and holy, who didst command light to shine out of darkness, who hast given us rest in sleep, and hast raised us up to glorify Thee and to declare Thy goodness; we beseech Thee of Thy great mercy to accept us who now worship before Thee, and according to our power do give Thee thanks, and to grant unto us our requests for all things needful for the present life and for our everlasting salvation; through Jesus Christ our Lord.

Amen.

The Confession.

If we say we have no sin, we deceive ourselves, and the truth is not in us. If we confess our sins, Thou art faithful and just to forgive us our sins, and to cleanse us from all unrighteousness.

Almighty and most merciful Father, we have erred and strayed from Thy ways like lost sheep. We have followed too much the devices and desires of our own hearts. We have offended against Thy holy laws. We have left undone those things which we ought to have done, and we have done those things which we ought not to have done; and there is no health in us. But Thou, O Lord, have mercy upon us, miserable

offenders. Spare Thou them, O God, which confess their faults. Restore Thou them that are penitent; according to Thy promises declared unto mankind in Christ Jesus our Lord. And grant, O most merciful Father, for His sake, that we may hereafter live a godly, righteous, and sober life, to the glory of Thy holy name.
Amen.

For Pardon and Peace.

Almighty God, the Father of our Lord Jesus Christ, who desirest not the death of a sinner, but rather that he may turn from his wickedness and live; and who pardonest and absolvest all them that truly repent, and unfeignedly believe His holy Gospel, we beseech Thee to grant us true repentance and Thy Holy Spirit, that those things may please Thee which we do at this present; and that the rest of our life hereafter may be pure and holy, so that at the last we may come to Thine eternal joy; through Jesus Christ our Lord. *Amen.*

Supplications.

O Almighty God, who, by Thy holy apostle, hast called upon us to present our bodies unto Thee a living sacrifice, holy and acceptable, which is our reasonable service; we come unto Thee in the name of Jesus Christ, and we devote and dedicate ourselves wholly to Thy service, henceforth to live only to Thy glory. Thou art our God, and we will praise Thee; Thou art our God, we will exalt Thee.

Enable us to be faithful to every trust which Thou in Thy providence hast committed to us, to discharge rightly the duties of our several relations in life, and to walk in Thy commandments and ordinances blameless.

Pour out upon us the gifts of the Holy Ghost. Grant unto us faith unfeigned, a just and humble hope, and a never-failing charity. Grant unto us the grace of true humility, a meek and quiet spirit, and a holy and edifying conversation.

Grant unto us grace to deny ourselves; to bear one another's burdens; to be helpers of one another's joys; to be slow to anger; to fight manfully the battles of the Lord against the devil, the world, and the flesh; to redeem the time; and to walk always as in Thy presence.

Grant unto us moderation in all things; in mirth let us not be vain; in knowledge not puffed up; in zeal not bitter; and let us use the world as not abusing it, remembering that the fashion of this world passeth away.

Grant unto us spiritual wisdom, that we may discern what is pleasing to Thee, and follow what belongs to our peace; and let the knowledge and love of Thee and of Jesus Christ our Lord be our guide and our portion all our days. Sanctify us in spirit, soul, and body, and preserve us blameless unto the coming of our Lord and King.

Here may be introduced any other subject for Supplication.

Incline Thine ear to our prayers, we beseech Thee, through Jesus Christ, in whose name we further pray:

The Lord's Prayer.

(To be said by both Minister and Congregation.)

Our Father which art in heaven, Hallowed be Thy name. Thy kingdom come. Thy will be done in earth, as it is in heaven. Give us this day our daily bread. And forgive us our trespasses, as we forgive them that trespass against us. And lead us not into temptation; but deliver us from evil: For Thine is the kingdom, the power, and the glory, for ever and ever. **Amen.**

Here, and at the end of all the other Prayers, the Congregation say AMEN.

Then likewise shall be said—

O Lord, open Thou our lips:
And our mouth shall show forth Thy praise.

Then shall be said or sung a portion of the Psalter, ending with—

Glory be to the Father, and to the Son, and to the Holy Ghost:

As it was in the beginning, is now, and ever shall be, world without end. **Amen.**

Then shall be read a Lesson from the Old Testament, before which shall be said—

Hear the word of the Lord as it is written in   , chapter   , at the   verse.

Then shall be sung the Hymn TE DEUM LAUDAMUS *or other Hymn or Psalm, after which shall be read a Lesson from the New Testament, before which shall be said—*

Hear again the word of the Lord as it is written in   , chapter   , at the   verse.

At the end of the Lesson shall be said—

The Lord bless to us the reading of His word, and to His name be glory and praise. **Amen.**

Then shall be sung the Hymn BENEDICTUS *or other Hymn or Psalm, after which may be sung or said by the Minister and people standing—*

II.

The Apostles' Creed.

I BELIEVE in God the Father Almighty, Maker of heaven and earth:

And in Jesus Christ His only Son our Lord, who was conceived by the Holy Ghost, born of the Virgin Mary, suffered under Pontius Pilate, was crucified, dead, and buried: He descended into hell; the third day He rose again from the dead; He ascended into heaven, and sitteth on the right hand of God the Father Almighty; from thence He shall come to judge the quick and the dead.

I believe in the Holy Ghost; the holy Catholic Church; the communion of saints; the forgiveness of sins; the resurrection of the body; and the life everlasting. **Amen.**

The Lord be with you:
And with thy spirit.

Then, the Congregation kneeling, the Minister shall say—

Let us Pray.

Intercessions.

O God, who hast taught us to make supplications, prayers, intercessions, and giving of thanks for all men, we humbly beseech Thee to receive these our prayers which we offer to Thy divine majesty.

Remember in Thy mercy all men whom Thou hast made of one blood to dwell on the face of the earth, and deliver them from those evils and miseries by which any of them are oppressed; especially from ignorance, error, and unbelief, and from the bondage of sin. Cause Thy way to be known upon earth, Thy saving health among all nations: and hasten the time when the lost sheep of the house of Israel, together with the fulness of the Gentiles, shall be brought into the fold of Jesus Christ, the Shepherd and Bishop of our souls.

Almighty and most merciful Father, who hast loved Thy people with an everlasting love, and purchased them unto Thyself with the blood of Thy dear Son; favourably regard, we beseech Thee, Thy Church and congregation, and confirm them evermore with all spiritual gifts. Endue Thy ministering servants with wisdom and faith, with love and zeal, that they may diligently and wisely perform the work of the Lord to which they are called. And grant that the whole company of the faithful may be steadfast in the faith, abounding in hope, of one heart and of one mind, and filled with joy and with the Holy Ghost. **Amen.**

Remember in Thy mercy her most sacred Majesty the Queen; preserve her person in health and honour, her crown in wealth and dignity, her dominions in peace and plenty: keep her perpetually in Thy fear and favour, and crown her with glory, honour, and immortality.

Make Thy blessing also to rest upon Albert Edward Prince of Wales, the Princess of Wales, and all the members of the Royal Family.

We pray for the Queen's ministers and counsellors [for the High Court of Parliament at this time assembled], for the judges, and magistrates [especially the magistrates of this town], and all who are in authority: enlighten and guide them; and so dispose the affairs of this nation that righteousness and truth, peace and contentment, may everywhere prevail.

We commend to Thine almighty guardianship our Navy and Army, and all who are exposed to danger by sea or by land. **Amen.**

Remember in Thy mercy the poor and needy, the widow and the fatherless, the stranger and the friendless, the sick and the dying [and any such known to ourselves whom we name in our hearts before Thee]: relieve their needs, sanctify their sufferings, strengthen their weakness, and in due time bring them out of bondage into the glorious liberty of the sons of God.

Regard with Thy favour our kindred and all who are dear to us. Unite us in the bonds of a common faith and hope; and inspire us with mutual love, gentleness, and forbearance, that we may walk before Thee in our homes with a perfect heart.

Eternal God, with whom do rest the spirits of just men made perfect; we bless and praise Thy holy name for all Thy servants departed this life in Thy faith and fear; and especially for those most dear to us who have fallen asleep in Jesus. And we beseech Thee to give us grace so to follow their good example, that we may continue united to them in fellowship of spirit, and that finally we may be gathered together in Thy heavenly kingdom, through Jesus Christ our Lord. **Amen.**

Then a Psalm or Hymn is sung, or, when convenient, the Anthem.

Then, the Congregation kneeling, the Minister shall say—

Let us Pray.

III.

The Thanksgiving.

WE will extol Thee, O God, our King;
And we will bless Thy name for ever and ever.

We give thanks unto Thee, O God of our salvation, that Thou hast crowned our lives with Thy goodness, and that by Thy blessing we, and all things living, are nourished and sustained. Thou hast preserved us all our days, and now again Thou bringest us into Thy presence, in the multitude of Thy mercies, and replenished with Thy goodness.

Above all, Thou hast loved us and all mankind when we were lost and undone; and hast given Thine only-begotten Son to seek and save us. We bless Thee for His great love to us, for His unspotted holiness, for His perfect example, for His bitter passion, and His death upon the cross, for His triumph over death and hell, for His glorious resurrection and ascension, for His intercession and rule at Thy right hand. We thank Thee for the giving of the Holy Ghost; for the Church which Thou hast planted among men; for its ministries and means of grace; for the promises and precepts of Thy holy Word; and for all the helps and comforts of true religion.

Here may be introduced any other subject for Thanksgiving.

Help us with our whole soul evermore to praise Thee, and to live worthy of these Thy benefits; through Jesus Christ our Lord. **Amen.**

Here followeth the Prayer for Illumination, in these words, or at the discretion of the Minister.

For Illumination.

O Lord and lover of men, cause the pure light of Thy divine knowledge to shine forth in our hearts, and open the eyes of our understandings that we may comprehend the precepts of Thy Gospel. Plant in us also the fear of Thy blessed commandments; that we, subduing all fleshly

IV.

Prayer after Sermon.

FATHER of mercies, and God of all comfort, we joyfully acknowledge Thine infinite goodness in sending to us the day-spring from on high to enlighten our darkness, and guide our feet into the way of peace. We praise Thy name for those portions of Thy holy Word of which Thou hast made us partakers this day. Grant that they may bring forth fruit unto holiness in our whole life, to the glory of Thy name, the edification of our brethren, and the comfort of our souls in the day of our Lord Jesus Christ. **Amen.**

Here may be introduced any special Prayers, as occasion may require.

O Lord Jesus Christ, who hast died for us, that whether we wake or sleep, we should live together with Thee; be Thou our strength every morning, and our rest when the shadows of the evening are stretched out, O Jesus Christ, our Lord. **Amen.**

Then the Offering is collected; a Psalm or Hymn is sung; and the Minister closes the service by pronouncing one or other of these Benedictions—

The grace of our Lord Jesus Christ, and the love of God, and the communion of the Holy Ghost, be with you all. **Amen.**

Or—

The peace of God, which passeth all understanding, keep your hearts and minds in the knowledge and love of God, and of His Son Jesus Christ, our Lord; and the blessing of God Almighty, the Father, the Son, and the Holy Ghost, be amongst you, and remain with you always. **Amen.**

Fourth Sunday of the Month.

Morning Service.

The Congregation being assembled, Divine Service may begin with the singing of a Psalm or Hymn; then, the Congregation still standing, the Minister shall say—

THE sacrifices of God are a broken spirit; a broken and a contrite heart, O God, Thou wilt not despise.

Offer the sacrifices of righteousness, and put your trust in the Lord.

Then, the Congregation kneeling, the Minister shall say—

Let us Pray.

I.

Prayer of Invocation.

O GOD, the Father of our Lord and Saviour Jesus Christ, the mighty God, who art blessed for evermore, we Thy people and the sheep of Thy pasture draw near to Thee with reverence and godly fear.

Look down from heaven, in Thy tender love, on us approaching Thee through Thine Anointed, and sanctify our souls and bodies by Thy holy Spirit, and strengthen our infirmity, that our prayers may go up before Thee as incense, and be accepted as a sweet savour, through the same Jesus Christ our Lord.

The Confession.

If we say we have no sin, we deceive ourselves, and the truth is not in us. If we confess our sins, Thou art faithful and just to forgive us our sins, and to cleanse us from all unrighteousness.

O most merciful Father, we acknowledge and confess that we have sinned against heaven and in Thy sight, and are not worthy to be called Thy children. We have all gone astray from Thy way like lost sheep, and have walked in counsels of our own. We have known to do good, but we have not done it; we have named the name of Christ, but have not departed from iniquity.

We repent, O Lord, and are sorry for our sins. We especially bewail before Thee those things which are the present burden of our heart and conscience. We cannot stand before Thee as our Judge, but we come to Thee as our

Saviour, hoping in Thy mercies, which are more than can be numbered.

Forsake us not, O God, who put our trust in Thee. Remember not against us former transgressions, but remember Thy tender mercies and Thy loving-kindnesses, which have been ever of old. And as Thou wast ever merciful to Thy people Israel, as often as they in penitence turned unto Thee, so do Thou show the like mercy unto us, with whom Thou hast made a better covenant, confirmed and sealed with the blood of Thy beloved Son. **Amen.**

For Pardon and Peace.

Blessed be Thy name, O Lord, that Thou dost, through the ordinances of Thy Church, seal to Thy people the remission of their sins; wherefore we beseech Thee to grant to all here present who truly repent, and are resolved to walk in newness of life, the comfortable assurance that their transgressions are forgiven, and to fill them with the peace that cometh from above. **Amen.**

Supplications.

O God, who hast from the beginning chosen us to salvation, through sanctification of the Spirit, and belief of the truth; grant that, pardoned through Christ, and risen with Him, we may have our affections set upon things above, and may overcome the world with the victory of faith.

Take away from us, we beseech Thee, whatever is depraved and perverse, whatever is contrary to salvation, whatever is hurtful to the soul, and whatever is displeasing to Thee.

From the lust of the flesh, the lust of the eye, and the pride of life, good Lord, deliver us; and strengthen us, by the grace of Thy Holy Spirit, to fight the good fight of the faith, to endure hardness as good soldiers of Jesus Christ, to rule our bodies by temperance and our spirits by meekness, and to glorify Thee both with body and spirit which Thou hast redeemed. Amen.

O Thou great Master and Lord, whose are all things in heaven and earth, and who givest to every one as it seemeth good in Thy sight; grant us grace so to use the talents which Thou hast committed to us for a season, that when the Lord shall return to reckon with His servants, we may be enabled to give in our account with joy, and not with grief.

Almighty God, whose eternal providence is over all Thy works, we beseech Thee to help and deliver us Thy servants in all time of our tribulation and adversity, and also in all time of our prosperity and wealth, that we be not overwhelmed with despondency and fear, or lifted up with presumption and pride; but that enjoying Thy bounties with humility and thankfulness, and bearing Thy chastening with faith and hope, we may endure unto the end; and having finished the work Thou hast given us to do, may, through Thy mercy, enter into the joy of our Lord. **Amen.**

Here may be introduced any other subject for Supplication.

O God, who hast chosen Zion as Thy rest for ever, and hast promised abundantly to bless her provision, and satisfy her poor with bread, to clothe her priests with salvation, and to cause her saints to shout aloud for joy; grant that we may receive out of Christ's fulness, and grace for grace; and being nourished by Thy word and sacraments, may be built up unto everlasting life.

These our humble supplications we offer unto Thee through Thine only-begotten Son, in whose name and words we yet further pray:

The Lord's Prayer.

(*To be said by both Minister and Congregation.*)

Our Father which art in heaven, Hallowed be Thy name. Thy kingdom come. Thy will be done in earth, as it is in heaven. Give us this day our daily bread. And forgive us our trespasses, as we forgive them that trespass against us. And lead us not into temptation; but deliver us from evil: For Thine is the kingdom, the power, and the glory, for ever and ever. **Amen.**

Here, and at the end of all the other Prayers, the Congregation say AMEN.

Then likewise shall be said—

O Lord, open Thou our lips:
And our mouth shall show forth Thy praise.

Then shall be said or sung a portion of the Psalter, ending with—

Glory be to the Father, and to the Son, and to the Holy Ghost:
As it was in the beginning, is now, and ever shall be, world without end. **Amen.**

Then shall be read a Lesson from the Old Testament, before which shall be said—

Hear the word of the Lord as it is written in   , chapter   , at the   verse.

Then shall be sung the Hymn TE DEUM LAUDAMUS *or other Hymn or Psalm, after which shall be read a Lesson from the New Testament, before which shall be said—*

Hear again the word of the Lord as it is written in   , chapter   , at the   verse.

At the end of each Lesson shall be said—

The Lord bless to us the reading of His word, and to His name be glory and praise. **Amen.**

Then shall be sung the Hymn BENEDICTUS *or other Hymn or Psalm, after which may be sung or said by the Minister and people standing—*

II.

The Apostles' Creed.

I BELIEVE in God the Father Almighty, Maker of heaven and earth:

And in Jesus Christ His only Son our Lord, who was conceived by the Holy Ghost, born of the Virgin Mary, suffered under Pontius Pilate, was crucified, dead, and buried: He descended into hell; the third day He rose again from the dead; He ascended into heaven, and sitteth on the right hand of God the Father Almighty; from thence He shall come to judge the quick and the dead.

I believe in the Holy Ghost; the holy Catholic Church; the communion of saints; the forgiveness of sins; the resurrection of the body; and the life everlasting. **Amen.**

The Lord be with you:
And with thy spirit.

Then, the Congregation kneeling, the Minister shall say—

Let us Pray.

Intercessions.

O God, who hast taught us to make supplications, prayers, intercessions, and giving of thanks for all men, we humbly beseech Thee to receive these our prayers which we offer to Thy divine majesty.

Almighty God, who hast made of one blood all nations, we pray for the peace of the whole world, and the salvation of all men. Look in pity upon Thine ancient people, whose are the fathers, and of whom according to the flesh Jesus Christ our Lord and Saviour came; and have mercy upon all who are in bondage to heathen superstition, and fetch them home, blessed Lord, to Thy flock, that they may be saved among the remnant of the true Israelites.

We pray especially for the good estate of the Catholic Church; that the divisions which desolate Thine heritage may be healed; that what is wanting anywhere may be supplied; and that every plant that is not of Thy planting may be rooted up.

We pray for all pastors and ministers of Thy Word, that they may take heed to themselves and to all the flocks over which the Holy Ghost deceitfulness of sin: vouchsafe them grace to come to themselves; the will and the power to return unto Thee; and the loving welcome of Thy forgiveness. **Amen.**

O Lord our heavenly Father, high and mighty, King of kings, Lord of lords, the only Ruler of princes, who dost from Thy throne behold all the dwellers upon earth; most heartily we beseech Thee with Thy favour to behold her most sacred Majesty Queen Victoria, and so replenish her with the grace of Thy Holy Spirit that she may always incline to Thy will, and walk in Thy way; endue her plenteously with heavenly gifts; grant her in health and wealth long to live; strengthen her that she may vanquish and overcome all her enemies; and finally, after this life, she may attain everlasting joy and felicity; through Jesus Christ our Lord.

Almighty God, the Fountain of all goodness, we humbly beseech Thee to bless Albert Edward Prince of Wales, the Princess of Wales, and all the Royal Family. Endue them with Thy Holy Spirit; enrich them with Thy heavenly grace; prosper them with all happiness; and bring them to Thine everlasting kingdom; through Jesus Christ our Lord.

We pray [for the High Court of Parliament now assembled, and] for all rulers, judges, and magistrates [especially for those of this town], that Thou wouldst give the spirit of wisdom to those to whom Thou hast given the authority of government; and for all ranks and conditions of men, that all may serve their generation in Thy fear. **Amen.**

We pray for all in sickness and distress [and for any such known to ourselves whom we name in our hearts before Thee]; that Thou wouldst give strength to the weary, aid to the sufferers, comfort to the sad, and help to all in tribulation.

We pray for the dying, that the souls of Thy servants may be released in peace, and that, departing from this world, they may live for evermore with Thee.

And O, most loving Father, we remember with undying affection those near and dear to us whom death has taken, and who rest from their earthly labours and sleep in Jesus. United still in one household of faith and love, may we live in the blessed hope, that when the day of God shall dawn and the shadows flee away, we shall meet with them and all Thy redeemed in Thy presence where there is fulness of joy, through Jesus Christ our Lord. **Amen.**

Then a Psalm or Hymn is sung, or, when convenient, the Anthem.

Then, the Congregation kneeling, the Minister shall say—

Let us Pray.

III.

The Thanksgiving.

O GOD, according to Thy name, so is Thy praise unto the ends of the earth:
In goodness art Thou exalted, O Lord our Father, for ever and for ever.

We magnify Thee, we praise Thee, we worship Thee; we give thanks unto Thee for Thy good providence, for all the blessings of the present life, and all the hopes of a better life to come. We thank Thee for the preservation of our lives, and the bountiful supply of our returning wants, for health of body and soundness of mind, for strength and skill to labour in our several callings, and for that portion of earthly good which Thou hast bestowed upon us. We thank Thee for loving parents, for faithful pastors and teachers, for benefactors never to be forgotten, for kind friends, for brethren of one mind with us in the Lord, and for all who have helped us onwards in our heavenward way.

Above all, we praise and bless Thee for Thy Son our Saviour, for Thy Spirit our Sanctifier, for the ministration of Thy holy angels, for the example of Thy saints and martyrs, and for the hope of an eternal weight of glory.

Here may be introduced any other subject for Thanksgiving.

Let the memory of Thy goodness, we beseech Thee, fill our hearts with joy and thankfulness unto our life's end; and let these, our thanksgivings, go up with acceptance before Thy throne; through Jesus Christ our Lord.

Amen.

Then followeth the Prayer for Illumination, in these words, or at the discretion of the Minister.

For Illumination.

Almighty God, with whom are hid all the treasures of wisdom and knowledge, open our eyes that we may behold wondrous things out of Thy law, and give us grace that we may clearly understand and heartily choose the way of Thy commandments; through Jesus Christ our Lord.

Then may be sung a Psalm or Hymn.
A Sermon is then preached, concluding with an Ascription of Praise; after which the Minister shall say—

Let us Pray.

IV.

Prayer after Sermon.

LORD of all power and might, who art the Author and Giver of all good things; graft in our hearts the love of Thy name; increase in us true religion ; nourish us with all goodness ; and of Thy great mercy keep us in the same ; through Jesus Christ our Lord.

Here may be introduced any special Prayers, as occasion may require.

Lighten our darkness, we beseech Thee, O Lord, and by Thy great mercy defend us from all perils and dangers of this night; for the love of Thy only Son our Saviour, Jesus Christ.

Then the Offering is collected; a Psalm or Hymn is sung; and the Minister closes the service by pronouncing one or other of these Benedictions—

The grace of our Lord Jesus Christ, and the love of God, and the communion of the Holy Ghost, be with you all. **Amen.**

Or—

The peace of God, which passeth all understanding, keep your hearts and minds in the knowledge and love of God, and of His Son Jesus Christ, our Lord; and the blessing of God Almighty, the Father, the Son, and the Holy Ghost, be amongst you, and remain with you always. **Amen.**

Fifth Sunday of the Month.

Morning Service.

The Congregation being assembled, Divine Service may begin with the singing of a Psalm or Hymn; then, the Congregation still standing, the Minister shall say—

IF ye, being evil, know how to give good gifts unto your children, how much more shall your Father which is in heaven give good things to them that ask Him?

Ask, and it shall be given you: seek and ye shall find: knock and it shall be opened unto you.

Then, the Congregation kneeling, the Minister shall say—

Let us Pray.

I.

Prayer of Invocation.

ALMIGHTY God our heavenly Father, who hast permitted us again to assemble in Thy house of prayer, give us grace, we humbly beseech Thee, to draw near to Thee in purity and sincerity of heart, and to offer unto Thee the sacrifices of prayer and praise with unfeigned self-devotion: and may it please Thee to make Thyself known to us, and to satisfy us with Thy mercy; through Jesus Christ our Lord. **Amen.**

The Confession.

Almighty and most merciful Father, who callest the sinner to forsake his way and to return unto Thee that Thou mayest have mercy upon him, we humbly acknowledge before Thee our manifold sins and shortcomings. We have grievously sinned against Thee in thought and word and deed. We have broken Thy holy commandments and have departed from Thy ways. We have been unthankful for Thy mercies, we have despised Thy fatherly goodness, we have resisted and grieved Thy Holy Spirit. We have not fulfilled the law of Christ that we should bear one another's burdens. We have not loved our neighbour as ourselves; we have not done unto others as we would that they should do unto us; we have sought too much our own gain and advantage, and have closed our hearts against our fellow-men, forgetting that we are members one of another.

For Pardon and Peace.

But Thou, O God, have mercy upon us Thy penitent children, and grant us Thy forgiveness through Jesus Christ our Lord.

Turn us again unto Thyself, and suffer us not to fall away from Thee, for with Thee there is mercy, and Thou dost redeem Thy people from all their iniquities.

O Thou who didst send Thy son Jesus Christ into the world to seek and to save that which was lost, receive us in Thy mercy and comfort us with Thy salvation.

Create in us a clean heart, O God:
And renew a right spirit within us.
Cast us not away from Thy presence:
And take not Thy Holy Spirit from us.

Amen.

Supplications.

Hear, O Lord, our humble supplications.

Almighty God, our heavenly Father, who of Thine infinite compassion hast brought us to Thyself, and given us peace with Thee through Jesus Christ our Lord, grant that with all our heart and soul we may love Thee who hast so loved us, and that with all our powers we may show forth Thy praise.

Take us, we entreat Thee, under Thy heavenly guidance and protection: deliver us from all unbelief and hardness of heart, give us a simple and childlike faith in Thy goodness and love, and in all things lead and direct us by Thy Holy Spirit.

Unite us by a true and living faith to Christ our Saviour, that we may know the fellowship of His sufferings and the power of His resurrection; and grant that, denying ourselves, and following in the footsteps of our Lord, we may grow into His likeness, and be made partakers of His joy.

Kindle in us such love towards our fellow-men that we may live in charity and peace with all the world; and, as Christ pleased not Himself, but gave Himself for us, so grant that we may devote ourselves with cheerfulness and zeal to the service and welfare of our brethren.

O God who art light, and in whom is no darkness at all, shine into our minds, we beseech Thee, with the knowledge of Thyself, and incline our hearts to understanding. Grant to us, we beseech Thee, that we may love the laws of Thy kingdom, and rejoice in the works which Thou hast made, that in Thy light we may see light, and in Thy service find perfect freedom.

Confirm and strengthen in us, O Lord, sincere and upright purposes, foster in us warm and true affections, and give us strength to bring to good effect the holy desires which by Thy grace arise in our hearts. When we are tempted strengthen

MORNING SERVICE.

us; when we are weak encourage us; when we are cast down raise us up. Leave us not without Thy grace, most merciful God, but perfect Thy work in us, and grant that we may do Thee true and faithful service in this world, and may enter at the last into Thy eternal peace; through Jesus Christ our Lord. **Amen.**

The Lord's Prayer.
(To be said by both Minister and Congregation.)

Our Father which art in heaven, Hallowed be Thy name. Thy kingdom come. Thy will be done in earth, as it is in heaven. Give us this day our daily bread. And forgive us our trespasses, as we forgive them that trespass against us. And lead us not into temptation; but deliver us from evil: For Thine is the kingdom, the power, and the glory, for ever and ever. **Amen.**

Here, and at the end of all the other Prayers, the Congregation say AMEN.

Then likewise shall be said—

O Lord, open Thou our lips:
And our mouth shall show forth Thy praise.

Then shall be said or sung a portion of the Psalter, ending with—

Glory be to the Father, and to the Son, and to the Holy Ghost:

As it was in the beginning, is now, and ever shall be, world without end. **Amen.**

Then shall be read a Lesson from the Old Testament, before which shall be said—

Hear the word of the Lord as it is written in   , chapter   , at the   verse.

Then shall be sung the Hymn TE DEUM LAUDAMUS *or other Hymn or Psalm, after which shall be read a Lesson from the New Testament, before which shall be said—*

Hear again the word of the Lord as it is written in   , chapter   , at the   verse.

At the end of each Lesson shall be said—

The Lord bless to us the reading of His word, and to His name be glory and praise. **Amen.**

Then shall be sung the Hymn BENEDICTUS *or other Hymn or Psalm.*

Then, the Congregation kneeling, the Minister shall say—

Let us Pray.

II.

Intercessions.

O GOD, the Father of all mankind, who art good to all, and whose tender mercies are over all Thy works, hear us as we pray for the well-being of all men, beseeching Thee to make Thy way known upon earth, and Thy saving health among all nations.

Bless abundantly, O Lord, the Church of Christ which Thou hast called out of the world, that she might bring the world to Thee; grant to her security and peace, heal her divisions, remove from her all superstition, error, and unbelief, purify her from every stain, and enable her so to follow her blessed Lord that she may abound in good works, and shed over the world the pure light of Christ.

Bless, O Lord, this parish and congregation. Grant that Christ may be manifested in Thy people in this place; as the gospel of peace has entered into their ears, so let all enmity be removed from their hearts and from their conversation; and let them lift up to Thee unceasingly the daily sacrifice of prayer and thankfulness and of good works.

Remember, O Lord, for good all ministers, pastors, and teachers, all who preach the gospel among the heathen, and all who serve Thee in any office in Thy Church.

O Lord, save Thy people:
And bless Thy heritage.
Govern them also:
And lift them up for ever.

O Father of Lights and Fountain of all knowledge, bless, we beseech Thee, all schools, universities, and places of learning, and grant that from them the light of truth may shine with growing brightness on all men, so that wisdom and knowledge may be the stability of our times.

O God, who dost appoint to every man his work, prosper, we pray Thee, the efforts of all who serve Thee in science, art, and letters, and of all those who seek to make the lives of Thy children brighter and happier. And in whatever occupation Thy people serve Thee faithfully, grant them to know that their labour is not in vain in the Lord. **Amen.**

O Thou by whom kings reign and princes decree justice, we pray Thee to regard with Thy favour all rulers and princes. Bless Thy servant, our sovereign, Queen Victoria; grant that her reign may be holy and peaceable, and save her from all her enemies. Bless Albert Edward Prince of Wales, the Princess of Wales, and all the Royal Family, enduing them plentifully with the grace and virtue befitting their high station. Bless her Majesty's Ministers [the Houses of Parliament now assembled], and all judges and magistrates [especially the magistrates of this town]. Grant to them wisdom and faith, guide their counsels, prosper their rule. Bless, O Lord, the Army and Navy; may it please Thee to support them in all hardships, and to grant them defence and deliverance in all perils. **Amen.**

We remember before Thee, O Lord, our brethren who are tried with sickness: entreating Thee to increase their faith and patience, to restore them to health, if it be Thy will, and to give them a happy issue out of all their troubles.

We remember before Thee all physicians, and nurses of the sick, those who have the care of young children, and those who tend the aged and infirm; and we beseech Thee to visit them with Thy comfort and aid, and to reward them for their work of patience and labour of love.

Have pity on all widows and orphans; succour all who are in danger by sea and land, and have mercy on all prisoners and captives, and on all who are oppressed with labour and toil. Have mercy on those who are tempted, and on those who are in darkness and perplexity, and strengthen them with Thy Holy Spirit. Be present with those who are dying, and grant that they may depart in peace, fearing no evil, and live before Thee in Thy heavenly kingdom.

We remember before Thee with grateful hearts Thy faithful servants who have departed this life in Thy love and fear. We praise and thank Thee for all who have been to us apostles and teachers, for those who have guided and defended us, for those who have loved us and have done us good.

We praise Thee for Thy gifts bestowed upon them, and for the rest into which they have entered, whereunto we pray that we also may in due time attain; through Jesus Christ our Lord.   **Amen.**

Then a Psalm or Hymn is sung, or, when convenient, the Anthem.

Then, the Congregation kneeling, the Minister shall say—

Let us Pray.

III.

The Thanksgiving.

O MAGNIFY the Lord with me:
Let us exalt His name together.

Almighty God, whom all Thy works throughout all places of Thy dominion praise continually, accept, we pray Thee, the thanks which we offer Thee for all Thy goodness. We praise Thee for all the works of Thy hands, O Thou Creator and Governor of all things. We bless Thee that Thou hast created us in Thine own image, that Thou hast revealed to us Thy counsels, and hast made us partakers of Thy thoughts, and fellow-workers in Thy kingdom. We praise Thee that Thou hast never left Thyself without a witness in the world, and that Thou hast spoken to us at sundry times and in divers manners by Thy prophets. Especially we praise Thee that in the fulness of time Thou didst send forth Thy Son, the brightness of Thy glory, and the express image of Thy person. We bless Thee that in Him the true light has come into the world, to deliver us from darkness, and to lead us into heavenly truth. We praise Thee that in Him we have the forgiveness of our sins, and that Thou hast sent us Thy Holy Spirit to bear witness with our spirits that we are Thy children, and heirs of Thy kingdom. Thou hast never forsaken us, O God; Thou hast made goodness and mercy to follow us; Thou hast set open before us the gates of life. Grant, O Lord, that Thy grace and loving-kindness may dwell for ever in our hearts, and that all our life long we may show forth Thy praise.

Here may be introduced any other subject for Thanksgiving.

Accept, O Lord, the prayers and thanksgivings of Thy people; bestow upon us what Thou seest to be good for us, and grant that we may know the fulness of the blessing which Thou hast given us of Thine infinite mercy in Jesus Christ our Lord. **Amen.**

Then followeth the Prayer for Illumination, in these words, or at the discretion of the Minister.

For Illumination.

O God, who guidest the meek in judgment, and teachest them Thy way, we beseech Thee to give unto us Thy Holy Spirit and the wisdom that cometh from above: grant that Thy word may have free course and be glorified; may we receive it, as is meet, with joy and thankfulness, and be strengthened and purified thereby; so that with steadfast faith we may serve Thee who art invisible, and abide to our life's end in Thy love and fear; through Jesus Christ our Lord. **Amen.**

Then may be sung a Psalm or Hymn.

A Sermon is then preached, concluding with an Ascription of Praise; after which the Minister shall say—

Let us Pray.

IV.

Prayer after Sermon.

O GOD, from whom all good things do come, who causest Thy sun to rise upon us and sendest us rain from heaven and fruitful seasons, be pleased to bestow upon us day by day what we require. Grant to each of us the strength he needs to accomplish his task; bless the work of our hands and of our minds, and give us grace to serve Thee in health and in sickness, in wealth and in poverty. Sanctify our joys and our trials, and enable us to seek first Thy kingdom and righteousness, and to believe that Thou wilt add to us all else that is good; through Jesus Christ our Lord. **Amen.**

Here may be introduced any special Prayers, as occasion may require.

Then the Offering is collected; a Psalm or Hymn is sung; and the Minister closes the service by pronouncing one or other of these Benedictions—

The grace of our Lord Jesus Christ, and the love of God, and the communion of the Holy Ghost, be with you all. **Amen.**

Or—

The peace of God, which passeth all understanding, keep your hearts and minds in the knowledge and love of God, and of His Son Jesus Christ, our Lord; and the blessing of God Almighty, the Father, the Son, and the Holy Ghost, be amongst you, and remain with you always. **Amen.**

Evening Service.

The Congregation being assembled, Divine Service may begin with the singing of a Psalm or Hymn; then, the Congregation still standing, the Minister shall say—

BECAUSE ye are sons, God hath sent forth the Spirit of His Son into your hearts, crying, Abba, Father.

I will arise and go to my Father, and will say unto Him, Father, I have sinned against Heaven and before Thee, and am no more worthy to be called Thy Son.

Then, the Congregation kneeling, the Minister shall say—

Let us Pray.

I.

Prayer of Invocation.

O ALMIGHTY God, from whom every good prayer cometh, and who pourest out on all who desire it the spirit of grace and supplication: deliver us when we draw nigh to Thee from coldness of heart and wanderings of mind; that with steadfast thoughts and kindled affections we may worship Thee in spirit and in truth; through Jesus Christ our Lord. **Amen.**

The Confession.

O God, who hast taught us that there is joy in heaven over one sinner that repenteth, accept, we beseech Thee, the confession of our sins which we now make to Thee. Father, we have sinned and have done evil in Thy sight; we have been disobedient and rebellious children, we have not loved Thee as we ought, but have broken Thy laws and been unthankful for Thy goodness. We have not loved our neighbour as ourselves, we have been selfish and unkind, we have forgotten the commandments of Christ our Master.

For Pardon and Peace.

Have mercy upon us, O God, according to Thy loving-kindness; pardon the sins we have committed this day, and remember not against us our former transgressions. Make Thy face to shine upon us; comfort us with Thy peace and love; and may it please Thee to show us the way of repentance, that in the time to come we may walk in the path of Thy commandments, and find in Thy service our chief joy; through Jesus Christ our Lord. **Amen.**

Supplications.

Hear, O Lord, our humble supplications.

O Thou who knowest what things we have need of before we ask, give us grace, we beseech Thee, to seek first Thy kingdom and righteousness, and do Thou add to us all that is necessary for the body and for this present life. May we desire Thee more than all Thy gifts, that so desiring we may seek Thee, and seeking Thee may find Thee.

We beseech Thee to hear us, good Lord.

Quench in us, O Thou Lord of our life, all wrong desires, and preserve us from vanity and inconstancy, from foolish thoughts and impure affections.

We beseech Thee to hear us, good Lord.

Deliver us from selfishness and pride, from sloth and idleness, from narrowness of mind and hardness of heart.

We beseech Thee to hear us, good Lord.

Cleanse our hearts from anger, malice, and envy, from covetousness and greed, and from all the fleshly lusts that war against the soul.

We beseech Thee to hear us, good Lord.

Fill our hearts, we beseech Thee, with the grace of Thy Holy Spirit; make us kind, long-suffering, and gentle; give us grace to deny ourselves, and to submit to Thy holy will, and cheerfully to serve our brethren as we have opportunity.

We beseech Thee to hear us, good Lord.

Give us grace at all times to be lovers of truth, and servants of righteousness; deliver us from the fear of man and from all superstition and hypocrisy, that we may be the children of the light and of the day.

We beseech Thee to hear us, good Lord.

In adversity help us to be patient; in prosperity keep us humble; and when we cannot see the way before us, may we yet fear no evil, knowing that Thou art with us.

We beseech Thee to hear us, good Lord.

Establish us in truth and goodness by the inspiration of Thy Holy Spirit; that which we know not do Thou reveal, that which is lacking to us do Thou supply. Let Thy grace be sufficient for us, and Thy strength be made perfect in our weakness.

We beseech Thee to hear us in all these our prayers: through Jesus Christ our Lord.

Amen.

The Lord's Prayer.

(*To be said by both Minister and Congregation.*)

Our Father which art in heaven, Hallowed be Thy name. Thy kingdom come. Thy will

FIFTH SUNDAY OF THE MONTH.

be done in earth, as it is in heaven. Give us this day our daily bread. And forgive us our trespasses, as we forgive them that trespass against us. And lead us not into temptation; but deliver us from evil: For Thine is the kingdom, the power, and the glory, for ever and ever. **Amen.**

Here, and at the end of all the other Prayers, the Congregation say AMEN.

Then likewise shall be said—

Praise ye the Lord:
The Lord's name be praised.

Then shall be said or sung a portion of the Psalter, ending with—

Glory be to the Father, and to the Son, and to the Holy Ghost:
As it was in the beginning, is now, and ever shall be, world without end. **Amen.**

Then shall be read a Lesson from the Old Testament, before which shall be said—

Hear the word of the Lord as it is written in   , chapter   , at the   verse.

Then shall be sung the Hymn MAGNIFICAT *or other Hymn or Psalm, after which shall be read a Lesson from the New Testament, before which shall be said—*

Hear again the word of the Lord as it is written in   , chapter   , at the   verse.

At the end of each Lesson shall be said—

The Lord bless to us the reading of His word, and to His name be glory and praise.   **Amen.**

Then shall be sung the Hymn NUNC DIMITTIS *or other Hymn or Psalm.*

Then, the Congregation kneeling, the Minister shall say—

Let us Pray.

II.

Intercessions.

O LORD, who hast commanded us to make prayers and intercessions for all men,
We beseech Thee to bless all nations with unity, peace, and concord, and to cause light and freedom to arise, and to increase in the whole earth.

Visit with heavenly blessings the Church of Christ which Thou hast called in all lands to bear witness of Thy grace, and bless her in all her gates with abundance of charity and peace.

May it please Thee to illuminate all pastors and ministers of Thy Church with knowledge and understanding of the truth, that Thy people may be led in the green pastures of Thy word.

Teach, O Lord, all teachers of mankind; prosper all science and discovery, and cause art and learning to flourish. Cause Thy face to shine on all men; bless the labour of the husbandman, and prosper all lawful trades and industries.

Bless, we entreat Thee, all who bear rule upon the earth. Regard with Thy favour Her Majesty Queen Victoria, Albert Edward Prince of Wales, the Princess of Wales, and all the Royal Family.

Bless all rulers, judges, and magistrates, and grant that they may maintain justice and equity, that Thy people may serve Thee without fear in holiness and righteousness.

Bless the whole nation; save us from strife and faction, from blindness of heart, from worldliness, and from unfaithfulness to the high trust which Thou hast committed to us.

We commend to Thee, O Lord, our kindred, our friends, our benefactors, and those among whom we dwell. Let peace be to our households, and let those who dwell therein be children of peace. Bless the young; let them grow in wisdom and stature, and in favour with God and man.

Have compassion, O Lord, on the sick, the poor, the desolate, and all who are afflicted and sorrowful. Inspire them with faith and hope, and draw near to them, O living God, to uphold, comfort, and save them.

Turn back them that wander, O Lord, and accept the penitence of those who turn to Thee: cause the light of the life eternal to rise upon their minds, and deliver them from the power of their sins.

O Lord most High, with Thy whole Church throughout the world we give Thee thanks for all Thy faithful servants, who having witnessed in their lives a good confession have left the light of their example to shine before Thy people on earth. Mercifully grant that by Thy fatherly blessing we may be enabled to follow them in all virtuous and godly living, and that hereafter we may be with them in Thy heavenly presence, whither Jesus the Forerunner is for us entered; to whom, with Thee, the Father, and the Holy Ghost, be glory evermore.

Amen.

Then a Psalm or Hymn is sung, or, when convenient, the Anthem.

Then, the Congregation kneeling, the Minister shall say—

Let us Pray.

III.

The Thanksgiving.

O GIVE thanks unto the Lord, for He is good:
For His mercy endureth for ever.

We magnify and praise Thy glorious name, O Lord God Almighty, for all Thy goodness to us. Thou hast opened Thy hand and hast supplied all our wants; Thou hast loaded us with Thy benefits, so that our cup runneth over. Like as a father pitieth his children, so hast Thou pitied us; Thou hast upheld us in the day of our distress, and made light to arise upon us when we were in darkness.

O Lord our God, the Giver of all good, we bless Thee for Thy never-failing mercy: for all the benefits we have received, for whatever good we may have done, for all Thy promises, and all our hopes of good to come: We thank Thee for loving parents, for wise teachers, for generous benefactors, for brethren of one mind with us, for good masters, for faithful servants; for all who by their words, or writings, or example, have cheered and strengthened us. We praise Thee that Thou didst send Thy Son Jesus Christ into the world, that whosoever believeth in Him might not perish but have everlasting life; and that in Him Thou hast come near to us, and dwelt among us, and caused us to dwell with Thee, and to be heirs of Thine eternal kingdom. By Thy tender mercy, O God, the dayspring from on high hath visited us, to give light to them that sat in darkness, to guide our feet into the way of peace.

Bless the Lord, O my soul, and all that is within me bless His holy name.

Bless the Lord, O my soul, and forget not all His benefits.

Here may be introduced any other subject for Thanksgiving.

Receive, O Lord, with compassionate kindness the prayers and supplications of Thy children. Lead us and guide us, O God, for in Thee do we put our trust; through Jesus Christ our Lord.

Amen.

Then followeth the Prayer for Illumination, in these words, or at the discretion of the Minister.

For Illumination.

Almighty God, who makest the blind to see and the lame to walk, and openest the prison to them that are bound, let Thy word come to us, we beseech Thee, with power to deliver us from evil habits, from prejudice, from the fear of man, and from every bondage in which we are entangled, that so we may walk at liberty in the ways of Thy commandments, through Jesus Christ our Lord. **Amen.**

Then may be sung a Psalm or Hymn.

A Sermon is then preached, concluding with an Ascription of Praise; after which the Minister shall say—

Let us Pray.

IV.

Prayer after Sermon.

O GOD, who hast appointed the day for labour and the night for rest, grant, we beseech Thee, that we may so rest in peace and quietness during the coming night, that afterward we may be able to go forth to our appointed labours. Take us into Thy holy keeping, so that no evil may befall us nor any plague come nigh our dwelling. Be pleased, O heavenly Father, to cover our sins with Thy mercy as Thou coverest the earth with the darkness of night, and grant that as our bodies are refreshed by quiet sleep, so also our souls may rest in the sense of Thy forgiveness and mercy.

We praise Thee, O God, that Thou hast not appointed us to wrath, but to obtain salvation by our Lord Jesus Christ, who died for us, that whether we wake or sleep we should live together

with Him. Help us, we pray Thee, with true faith to rest on Him, and all our life long with purpose of heart to cleave to Him. And when at length our days are ended and our work is finished in this world, grant that we may depart hence in the blessed assurance of Thy favour, and in the sure hope of that glorious kingdom where there is day without night, and light without darkness, and life without the shadow of death for ever, through Jesus Christ our Lord.
Amen.

Here may be introduced any special Prayers, as occasion may require.

Then the Offering is collected; a Psalm or Hymn is sung; and the Minister closes the service by pronouncing one or other of these Benedictions—

The grace of our Lord Jesus Christ, and the love of God, and the communion of the Holy Ghost, be with you all. **Amen.**

Or—

The peace of God, which passeth all understanding, keep your hearts and minds in the knowledge and love of God, and of His Son Jesus Christ, our Lord; and the blessing of God Almighty, the Father, the Son, and the Holy Ghost, be amongst you, and remain with you always. **Amen.**

Alternative Order of Service.

(Which may be adopted, if desired, in place of the foregoing.)

Invitatory Psalm.
Scripture Sentences.
Prayer: Invocation—Confession—For Pardon and Peace—Supplications.
Prose Psalter.
Lesson from Old Testament.
Psalm or Hymn.
Lesson from New Testament.
Praise.
Creed.
Prayer: Thanksgiving — Illumination — Lord's Prayer.
Sermon.
Prayer: Intercessions.
Praise.
Collection.
Praise.
Benediction.

Book of Common Order.

PART II.

CONTAINING ADDITIONAL MATERIALS FOR DAILY AND OTHER SERVICES

Contents.

		PAGE
I. THE LITANY	. . . .	179
II. PRAYERS, INTERCESSIONS, AND THANKSGIVINGS FOR SPECIAL OCCASIONS—		
PRAYERS AND INTERCESSIONS	. . . .	188
THANKSGIVINGS	. . . . .	209
III. PRAYERS FOR SPECIAL GRACES	. . .	213
IV. COLLECTS AND PRAYERS FOR NATURAL AND SACRED SEASONS	. . . .	231
V. ADDITIONAL FORMS OF SERVICE—		
INTRODUCTORY SENTENCES	. . . .	249
PRAYERS OF INVOCATION	. . . .	253
CONFESSIONS	. . . . . .	256
PRAYERS FOR PARDON AND PEACE	. . .	259
PRAYER OF DEDICATION	. . . .	261
SUPPLICATIONS	. . . . .	262
INTERCESSIONS	. . . . .	266
THANKSGIVINGS	. . . . .	276
PRAYERS FOR ILLUMINATION	. . .	278
PRAYERS AFTER SERMON	. . . .	279
ASCRIPTIONS OF GLORY	. . . .	282

I.

The Litany.

O GOD the Father, of heaven: have mercy upon us miserable sinners.
O God the Father, of heaven: have mercy upon us miserable sinners.

O God the Son, Redeemer of the world: have mercy upon us miserable sinners.
O God the Son, Redeemer of the world: have mercy upon us miserable sinners.

O God the Holy Ghost, proceeding from the Father and the Son: have mercy upon us miserable sinners.
O God the Holy Ghost, proceeding from the Father and the Son: have mercy upon us miserable sinners.

O holy, blessed, and glorious Trinity, three Persons and one God: have mercy upon us miserable sinners.
O holy, blessed, and glorious Trinity, three

Persons and one God: have mercy upon us miserable sinners.

Remember not, Lord, our offences, nor the offences of our forefathers; neither take Thou vengeance of our sins: spare us, good Lord; spare Thy people, whom Thou hast redeemed with Thy most precious blood, and be not angry with us for ever.

Spare us, good Lord.

From all evil and mischief; from sin, from the crafts and assaults of the devil; from Thy wrath, and from everlasting damnation,

Good Lord, deliver us.

From all blindness of heart; from pride, vainglory, and hypocrisy; from envy, hatred, and malice, and all uncharitableness,

Good Lord, deliver us.

From fornication, and all other deadly sin; and from all the deceits of the world, the flesh, and the devil,

Good Lord, deliver us.

From lightning and tempest; from plague, pestilence, and famine; from battle and murder, and from sudden death,

Good Lord, deliver us.

From all sedition, privy conspiracy, and rebellion; from all false doctrine, heresy, and schism; from hardness of heart, and contempt of Thy Word and Commandment,

Good Lord, deliver us.

By the mystery of Thy holy Incarnation; by Thy holy Nativity and Circumcision; by Thy Baptism, Fasting, and Temptation,
Good Lord, deliver us.

By Thine Agony and bloody Sweat; by Thy Cross and Passion; by Thy precious Death and Burial; by Thy glorious Resurrection and Ascension; and by the coming of the Holy Ghost,
Good Lord, deliver us.

In all time of our tribulation; in all time of our wealth; in the hour of death, and in the day of judgment,
Good Lord, deliver us.

We sinners do beseech Thee to hear us, O Lord God; and that it may please Thee to rule and govern Thy holy Church universal in the right way;
We beseech Thee to hear us, good Lord.

That it may please Thee to keep and strengthen in the true worshipping of Thee, in righteousness and holiness of life, Thy servant Victoria, our most gracious Queen and Governor;
We beseech Thee to hear us, good Lord.

That it may please Thee to rule her heart in Thy faith, fear, and love, and that she may evermore have affiance in Thee, and ever seek Thy honour and glory;
We beseech Thee to hear us, good Lord.

That it may please Thee to be her defender and keeper, giving her the victory over all her enemies;

We beseech Thee to hear us, good Lord.

That it may please Thee to bless and preserve Albert Edward Prince of Wales, the Princess of Wales, and all the Royal Family;

We beseech Thee to hear us, good Lord.

That it may please Thee to illuminate all Thy Ministers with true knowledge and understanding of Thy Word, and that both by their preaching and living they may set it forth, and show it accordingly;

We beseech Thee to hear us, good Lord.

That it may please Thee to endue the Lords of the Council, and all the Nobility, with grace, wisdom, and understanding;

We beseech Thee to hear us, good Lord.

That it may please Thee to bless and keep the Magistrates, giving them grace to execute justice, and to maintain truth;

We beseech Thee to hear us, good Lord.

That it may please Thee to bless and keep all Thy people;

We beseech Thee to hear us, good Lord.

That it may please Thee to give to all nations unity, peace, and concord;

We beseech Thee to hear us, good Lord.

That it may please Thee to give us an heart

to love and dread Thee, and diligently to live after Thy commandments;
We beseech Thee to hear us, good Lord.

That it may please Thee to give to all Thy people increase of grace to hear meekly Thy Word, and to receive it with pure affection, and to bring forth the fruits of the Spirit;
We beseech Thee to hear us, good Lord.

That it may please Thee to bring into the way of truth all such as have erred, and are deceived;
We beseech Thee to hear us, good Lord.

That it may please Thee to strengthen such as do stand; and to comfort and help the weak-hearted; and to raise up them that fall; and finally to beat down Satan under our feet;
We beseech Thee to hear us, good Lord.

That it may please Thee to succour, help, and comfort all that are in danger, necessity, and tribulation;
We beseech Thee to hear us, good Lord.

That it may please Thee to preserve all that travel by land or by water, all women labouring of child, all sick persons, and young children; and to show Thy pity upon all prisoners and captives;
We beseech Thee to hear us, good Lord.

That it may please Thee to defend, and provide for, the fatherless children, and widows, and all that are desolate and oppressed;

We beseech Thee to hear us, good Lord.

That it may please Thee to have mercy upon all men;

We beseech Thee to hear us, good Lord.

That it may please Thee to forgive our enemies, persecutors, and slanderers, and to turn their hearts;

We beseech Thee to hear us, good Lord.

That it may please Thee to give and preserve to our use the kindly fruits of the earth, so as in due time we may enjoy them;

We beseech Thee to hear us, good Lord.

That it may please Thee to give us true repentance; to forgive us all our sins, negligences, and ignorances; and to endue us with the grace of Thy Holy Spirit to amend our lives according to Thy holy Word;

We beseech Thee to hear us, good Lord.

Son of God: we beseech Thee to hear us.

Son of God: we beseech Thee to hear us.

O Lamb of God: that takest away the sins of the world;

Grant us Thy peace.

O Lamb of God: that takest away the sins of the world;

Have mercy upon us.

O Christ, hear us.

O Christ, hear us.

Lord, have mercy upon us.
Lord, have mercy upon us.
Christ, have mercy upon us.
Christ, have mercy upon us.
Lord, have mercy upon us.
Lord, have mercy upon us.

Then shall the Minister and the People with him say the Lord's Prayer.

Our Father which art in heaven, Hallowed be Thy name. Thy kingdom come. Thy will be done in earth, as it is in heaven. Give us this day our daily bread. And forgive us our trespasses, as we forgive them that trespass against us. And lead us not into temptation; but deliver us from evil. Amen.

O Lord, deal not with us after our sins.
Neither reward us after our iniquities.

O God, merciful Father, that despisest not the sighing of a contrite heart, nor the desire of such as be sorrowful; mercifully assist our prayers that we make before Thee in all our troubles and adversities, whensoever they oppress us; and graciously hear us, that those evils, which the craft and subtilty of the devil or man worketh against us, be brought to nought, and by the providence of Thy goodness they may be dispersed; that we Thy servants, being hurt by no persecutions, may evermore give thanks unto Thee in Thy holy Church; through Jesus Christ our Lord.

O Lord, arise, help us, and deliver us for Thy Name's sake.

O God, we have heard with our ears, and our fathers have declared unto us, the noble works that Thou didst in their days, and in the old time before them.

O Lord, arise, help us, and deliver us for Thine honour.

Glory be to the Father, and to the Son: and to the Holy Ghost.

As it was in the beginning, is now, and ever shall be: world without end. Amen.

From our enemies defend us, O Christ.

Graciously look upon our afflictions.

Pitifully behold the sorrows of our hearts.

Mercifully forgive the sins of Thy people.

Favourably with mercy hear our prayers.

O Son of David, have mercy upon us.

Both now and ever vouchsafe to hear us, O Christ.

Graciously hear us, O Christ; graciously hear us, O Lord Christ.

O Lord, let Thy mercy be showed upon us.

As we do put our trust in Thee.

We humbly beseech Thee, O Father, mercifully to look upon our infirmities; and for the glory of Thy Name turn from us all those evils that we most righteously have deserved; and grant, that in all our troubles we may put our whole trust and confidence in Thy mercy, and evermore serve Thee in holiness and pureness of living, to Thy honour and glory; through our only Mediator and Advocate, Jesus Christ our Lord. **Amen.**

Almighty God, who hast given us grace at this time with one accord to make our common supplications unto Thee; and dost promise, that when two or three are gathered together in Thy name, Thou wilt grant their requests: Fulfil now, O Lord, the desires and petitions of Thy servants, as may be most expedient for them; granting us in this world knowledge of Thy truth, and in the world to come life everlasting. **Amen.**

The grace of our Lord Jesus Christ, and the love of God, and the fellowship of the Holy Ghost, be with us all evermore. **Amen.**

II.

Prayers, Intercessions, and Thanksgivings for Special Occasions.

Prayers and Intercessions.

For Holy Communion.

1.

O GOD, Father of our Lord Jesus Christ, who dost, in Thy good providence, call us to draw near to Thee in Holy Communion; look graciously, we beseech Thee, upon Thy servants who are about to seek Thy grace in this most sacred ordinance. Give unto them true and hearty sorrow for past sins, power to confess the same unto Thee, grace to seek Thy mercy and forgiveness, and an earnest desire to walk before Thee in newness and holiness of life; and mercifully grant that we, with all those who shall come to Thy holy table, may be filled with Thy Spirit in the inner man; that drawing near with penitent hearts and lively faith, we may receive the holy sacrament to our present and everlasting comfort; through Thy Son our Saviour Jesus Christ. **Amen.**

2.

O God, who art the fountain of all holiness, we beseech Thee for the help of Thy continual grace; that, partaking of this Thy holy table as strangers and pilgrims here on earth, we may be advanced to partake of the heavenly feast in the general assembly of all Thy saints, in the day of Thy kingdom; through Jesus Christ our Lord, who liveth and reigneth with Thee, O Father, in the unity of the Holy Ghost, one God, world without end. **Amen.**

3.

O Lord Jesus Christ, who in Thy last supper with Thy disciples didst ordain in the blessed sacrament a perpetual memorial of Thy passion until Thy coming again; grant unto us, we beseech Thee, such discernment of Thy holy mysteries, that we may continually receive the full fruition of Thy redeeming love; who livest and reignest with the Father and the Holy Ghost, one God, world without end. **Amen.**

4.

O God, who, in these holy mysteries, hast vouchsafed to feed us with the spiritual food of the flesh and blood of Thy dear Son; we beseech Thee, that all who faithfully partake of the same may grow up in the communion of the body of Christ, and finally attain unto the glory of the resurrection; through the same Jesus Christ our Lord, who liveth and reigneth with Thee, O Father, in the unity of the Holy Ghost, one God, world without end. **Amen.**

Morning Prayers.

1.

From the night early awaketh our soul unto Thee, O God; for the light of Thy commandments is upon the earth. Teach us, O God, by Thy truth; by Thy commandments; by Thy judgments; enlighten the eyes of our minds lest we sleep the sleep of death. Remove from our hearts all darkness; give unto us the light of the Sun of righteousness; preserve our life free from all snares, by Thy Holy Spirit; and direct our footsteps in the way of peace; for Thine is the dominion, the power, and the glory, world without end. **Amen.**

2.

O God, who dividest the day from the night, separate our deeds from the gloom of darkness. As Thou hast awakened our bodies from sleep, so, we beseech Thee, awaken our souls from sin: as Thou hast caused the light of day to shine on our bodily eyes, cause the light of Thy Word and Holy Spirit to illuminate our hearts; and so give us grace, as the children of light, to walk in all holy obedience before Thy face this day, that in all our thoughts, words, and dealings, we may endeavour to keep faith and a clean conscience towards Thee and towards all men; through Jesus Christ our Lord. **Amen.**

3.

O Lord, our heavenly Father, almighty and everlasting God, who hast safely brought us to the beginning of this day, defend us in the same with Thy mighty power, and grant that this day we fall into no sin, neither run into any kind of danger, but that all our doings may be ordered by Thy governance to do always that is righteous in Thy sight; through Jesus Christ our Lord. **Amen.**

Evening Prayers.

1.

Blessed art Thou, O Lord, who hast granted us to pass through this day, and to reach the beginning of the night. Hear our prayers, and those of all Thy people; forgive us all our sins, negligences, and ignorances; accept our evening supplications, and send down on Thine inheritance the fulness of Thy mercy and compassion. Compass us about with Thy holy angels; arm us with the armour of Thy righteousness, and guard us by Thy power; deliver us from every assault and device of the adversary, and grant that we may pass this night and all the days and nights of our life in fulness of peace and holiness, without sin or offence; through Jesus Christ our Lord. **Amen.**

2.

O God, Most High, who alone art exalted, having immortality, and dwelling in the light which no one can approach unto; who hast given us grace to come before Thee at this time, to offer unto Thee our evening sacrifice of adoration and praise; grant unto us peace for the present evening and coming night; clothe us with the armour of light; save us from the fear of the night, and from all the perils of darkness; grant unto us sleep, that our weary bodies may be refreshed, and defend us from all the malice of the devil. And, O Lord, Giver of all good things, grant us, while resting on our beds, to remember Thy name in the silent watches of the night; which do Thou grant according to Thy good will towards us. And to Thee we ascribe glory; to the Father, and to the Son, and to the Holy Ghost, world without end. **Amen.**

3.

O God, who hast given the day to man for labour, and the night for rest, protect us by Thy watchful providence during the coming night, and all the nights and days of our pilgrimage. Cover all our sins with Thy mercy, as Thou coverest the earth with darkness during the night-watches. And when our days are ended, and our work is finished in this world, may we depart hence in the blessed assurance of Thy favour, and in the certain hope of the resurrection to immortal life, which Thou hast given us in our Lord and Saviour Jesus Christ. **Amen.**

4.

O God, with whom there is no darkness, but the night shineth as the day, keep and defend us, and all Thy saints, in soul and body, during the coming night. May we rest in the consciousness of Thy favour; in the peace of a good conscience; in the hope of a better life; in the faith of Thy providence; in the love of Thy Spirit.

May we rise up again to diligence in our several callings, to work the work of God while the day lasts, seeing the night cometh in which no man can work. And whether we wake or sleep, may we live together with Christ. **Amen.**

At Seed-time.

O Lord our God, author and giver of all good things, who hast ordained the earth to bring forth grass for cattle, and herbs and food for the service of man; look down in Thy compassion upon us, and bless, we beseech Thee, the labours of Thy servants, who till and sow the fields. Vouchsafe to us seasonable weather; cause Thy sun to shine, and let Thy rain and dew refresh the ground, that the fruits of the earth may be matured, our garners may be filled with corn and all good fruits, and that there may be abundance of food, both for man and for beast. So we Thy people and the sheep of Thy pasture will give Thee thanks for ever: we will show forth Thy praise to all generations. **Amen.**

For Rain.

O God, heavenly Father, who by Thy Son Jesus Christ hast promised to all them that seek

Thy kingdom and the righteousness thereof, all things necessary for their bodily sustenance; send us, we beseech Thee, in this our necessity, such moderate rain and showers, that we may receive the fruits of the earth to our comfort and to Thy honour; through Jesus Christ our Lord.
Amen.

In Time of a Rainy Harvest.

O God, our Sun and Shield, who hast spared us to see another season of ingathering, renew Thy mercy unto us, we beseech Thee, and stay the falling of the rain from heaven, that the increase which Thou hast given may not be destroyed. We confess that we have been worldly and thankless; and have forgotten that Thou, who crownest the year with Thy goodness, canst turn a fruitful land into barrenness for the wickedness of them that dwell therein. Hear our cry, O Lord, and have mercy upon us, that the fields may be joyful, and all that are therein. Let not the labour of the husbandman be in vain, O our Father: let not the bread of Thy children fail. But do Thou keep from all harm the fruits of the earth, till they be stored in our garners safely and in abundance. And this we ask for the sake of Him who fed the bodies of men with the bread that perisheth, and their souls with the living bread which came down from heaven. Amen.

In Time of Sickness.

Almighty God, who forgivest the iniquities of Thy people, and healest all their diseases; who hast proclaimed Thy name to be the Lord that healeth us, and hast sent Thy well-beloved Son to bear our sicknesses; look down upon us, Thine unworthy servants, who humble ourselves before Thee and acknowledge that we have justly provoked Thine anger. We beseech Thee to have mercy upon us, and to forgive us; and, of Thy loving-kindness, to remove this plague of sickness, the judgment of Thy hand, with which Thou hast visited us; and this we ask for the honour of Thy great name, through Jesus Christ our Lord. Amen.

On Behalf of Nations engaged in War.

O Lord God of infinite mercy, we humbly beseech Thee to look down upon the nations now engaged in war. Reckon not against Thy people their many iniquities, for from the lusts of our own hearts come wars and fightings amongst us. Look in mercy on those immediately exposed to peril, conflict, sickness, and death: comfort the prisoners, relieve the sufferings of the wounded, and show mercy to the dying. Remove in Thy good providence all causes and occasions of war; dispose the hearts of those engaged therein to moderation; and of Thy great goodness restore peace among the nations; through Jesus Christ our Lord. **Amen.**

In Time of War.

O Lord God of infinite mercy, we humbly beseech Thee to look down in compassion upon this kingdom and nation now involved in war. Reckon not against us our many iniquities; pardon our offences, our pride and arrogance, our self-sufficiency and forgetfulness of Thee.

Save and defend our gracious Queen. Give wisdom to her councillors, skill to her officers, courage and endurance to her soldiers and sailors. Look in mercy on those immediately exposed to peril, conflict, sickness, and death. Comfort the prisoners, relieve the sufferings of the wounded, and show mercy to the dying.

Finally, we beseech Thee to remove, in Thy good providence, all causes and occasions of war; to dispose our hearts and the hearts of our enemies to moderation; and of Thy great goodness to restore peace among the nations; through Jesus Christ our Lord. **Amen.**

To be used at Sea.

O eternal Lord God, who alone spreadest out the heavens and rulest the raging of the sea, and hast compressed the water within bounds, until day and night shall come to an end; be pleased to receive into Thine almighty and most gracious protection the persons of us Thy servants, and the ship [*or* fleet] in which we serve. Preserve us from dangers of the deep, and from the violence of enemies (that we may be a safeguard unto our country, and a security for such as do business in the mighty waters), that in due season we may return to our homes with a thankful remembrance of Thy mercies, and that finally, having passed the sea of this troubled life, we may enter the haven of eternal rest; through Him who is our only refuge and Saviour, Jesus Christ our Lord. Amen.

For Missions and Missionaries.

1.

O eternal Spirit, through whom in every nation he that feareth God and worketh righteousness is accepted before Him; enlighten our hearts that we may know and perceive, in all nations and kindreds of people, whatsoever there is in any of them of true and honest, just and pure, lovely and of good report; through the Word which lighteth every man, Jesus Christ our Lord.
Amen.

2.

O God, who hast made of one blood all nations of men to dwell on all the face of the earth, and didst send Thy blessed Son to preach peace to them that are afar off, and to them that are nigh; grant that all the people of heathen lands may seek after Thee and find Thee; and hasten, O Lord, the fulfilment of Thy promise to pour out Thy Spirit upon all flesh; through Jesus Christ our Lord. Amen.

3.

O God of Abraham, of Isaac, and of Jacob; have mercy, we beseech Thee, upon Thine ancient people the house of Israel; deliver them from their hardness of heart and unbelief of Thy Gospel, that, their hearts being turned to Thee, they may behold Thy glory in the face of Jesus Christ, and may acknowledge Him to be their Saviour, whom their fathers gave up to be crucified, so that they may be brought into Thy holy Church, and saved among the remnant of the true Israel; through Jesus Christ our Lord. Amen.

4.

O most merciful Saviour and Redeemer, who wouldst not that any should perish, but that all men should be saved and come to the knowledge of the truth; fulfil Thy gracious promise to be present with those who are gone forth in Thy name to preach the Gospel of salvation in distant lands. Be with them in all perils by land or by water, in sickness and distress, in weariness and painfulness, in disappointment and persecution. Bless them, we beseech Thee, with Thy continual favour; and send Thy Holy Spirit to guide them into all truth. O Lord, let Thy ministers be clothed with righteousness, and grant that Thy word spoken by their mouths may never be spoken in vain. Endue them with power from on high, and so prosper Thy work in their hands, that the fulness of the Gentiles may be gathered in, and all Israel be saved. Hear us, O Lord, for Thy mercy's sake, and grant that all who are called by Thy name may be one in Thee, and may abound more and more in prayers and offerings for the coming of Thy kingdom throughout the world, to Thy honour and glory, who livest and reignest with the Father and the Holy Ghost, ever one God, world without end. **Amen.**

5.

Almighty God, who by Thy Son Jesus Christ didst give commandment to the holy apostles that they should go into all the world and preach the Gospel to every creature; grant to us whom Thou hast called into Thy Church a ready will to obey Thy word, and fill us with a hearty desire to make Thy way known upon earth, Thy saving health among all nations. Look with compassion upon the heathen that have not known Thee, and on the multitudes that are scattered abroad as sheep having no shepherd. O heavenly Father, Lord of the harvest, have respect, we beseech Thee, to our prayers, and send forth labourers into Thine harvest. Fit and prepare them by Thy grace for the work of their ministry: give them the spirit of power, and of love, and of a sound mind: strengthen them to endure hardness; and grant that by their life and doctrine they may show forth Thy glory, and set forward the salvation of all men; through Jesus Christ our Lord.

Amen.

For our Fellow-Countrymen in Heathen Lands.

O Lord, who hast commanded us by Thine apostles to walk worthy of the vocation wherewith we are called, and as we have each received Thy gift, so to minister the same one to another; grant to all who are baptized into Thy holy name, and especially to our fellow-countrymen who sojourn in distant lands, that they may show forth Thy praises, who hast called them out of darkness into marvellous light. Preserve them, we beseech Thee, from the sin of offending Thy little ones who believe in Thee, and from causing Thy Word to be blasphemed among the heathen. Make them as the salt of the earth, and as a light in the world; that so, beholding their good works, and won by their holy life, multitudes may be turned to Thy truth, to glorify Thee in the day of visitation, who art our Saviour and our God, blessed for ever. Amen.

For such as offer themselves for, or are engaged in, works of Charity.

Almighty God, who didst send Thy Son Jesus Christ into the world, to visit us in our low estate, and to minister unto us Thy consolations; we render unto Thee our humble and hearty thanks that Thou hast inspired the hearts of these Thy servants with zeal for the honour of Thy name and desire to labour in Thy Church. And now we present them in Thy holy presence, and implore upon them the abundance of Thy grace and benediction. We pray Thee, shed abroad in their hearts Thy love, endow them with mercy and loving-kindness, with meekness and gentleness, with unwearying diligence and patient endurance. Grant them, O Lord, to persevere unto the end; and forget not, we beseech Thee, in that day, the work and labour of love which they shall have shown towards Thy holy name. May they be found at the right hand of Thy Son, and inherit the kingdom prepared for all who diligently serve Thee. Hear us for the sake of the same Jesus Christ our Lord; who liveth and reigneth with Thee, O Father, in the unity of the Holy Ghost, one God, world without end. Amen.

For a Blessing on Industrial Work done for the Church.

Almighty and most gracious God, Creator of all things, who hast given to us skill to devise, and also strength and ability to execute, and hast commanded us, whatsoever we do, to do all to Thy glory; prosper, we beseech Thee, our present labours, and grant that, ministering to Thy Church of our earthly things, we may receive from Thee an abundant increase of spiritual blessings, to the relief of our necessities and the glory of Thy grace; through Jesus Christ our Lord. Amen.

For Singers.

Almighty God, who hast ordained the faculties of man to be the eternal instruments of rendering to Thee glory and praise, and hast moved the hearts of these Thy servants to desire to serve Thee, in singing the praises of Thy name in the midst of Thy congregation; grant unto them, we beseech Thee, Thy blessing and grace. O Thou whose name is holy, who willest that all things in Thy house should be holiness unto Thee; sanctify these Thy servants, we humbly beseech Thee, in this holy work; endue them with the spirit of worship in Thy holy fear; that, through the presence and power of the Holy Ghost, they may edify themselves and all Thy congregation in psalms and hymns and spiritual songs, singing and making melody with grace in their hearts. Hear us, for the sake of Jesus Christ; to whom, with Thee and the Holy Ghost, be glory and praise for ever. Amen.

For Unity.

1.

O God, the Father of our Lord Jesus Christ, our only Saviour, the Prince of peace; give us grace seriously to lay to heart the great dangers we are in by our unhappy divisions. Take away all hatred and prejudice, and whatsoever else may hinder us from godly union and concord; that, as there is but one body, and one Spirit, and one hope of our calling, one Lord, one faith, one baptism, one God and Father of us all, so we may henceforth be all of one heart and of one soul, united in one holy bond of truth and peace, of faith and charity, and may with one mind and one mouth glorify Thee; through Jesus Christ our Lord. **Amen.**

2.

O Lord Jesus Christ, who saidst unto Thine apostles, Peace I leave with you, My peace I give unto you; regard not our sins, but the faith of Thy Church, and grant her that peace and unity which is agreeable to Thy will, who livest and reignest for ever and ever. **Amen.**

Almsgiving.

O Lord our Lord, who art King of all the earth; accept, of Thine infinite goodness, the offerings of Thy people, which, in obedience to Thy commandment, in honour of Thy name, and with a free will and joyful heart, we yield and dedicate to Thee: and grant unto us Thy blessing, that the same being devoted to Thy service, may be used for Thy glory, and for the welfare of Thy Church and people; through Jesus Christ our Lord. **Amen.**

Before Appointment of Office-Bearers.

Almighty God, the Giver of all good gifts, who by Thy Son Jesus Christ hast appointed diverse administrations for the edifying of His Body in truth, holiness, and charity; mercifully look upon Thy people whom Thou hast redeemed; and, at this time, so guide and govern them that they may faithfully and wisely make choice of fit *persons* to serve before Thee in Thy Church. And to *those* who shall be appointed to any holy function, give Thy grace and heavenly benediction, that both by *their* life and doctrine *they* may show forth Thy praise, and further the salvation of all men, to the glory of Thy great name, and the benefit of Thy holy Church, through Jesus Christ our Lord. 𝔄men.

For the General Assembly during its Session.

Almighty and everlasting God, who by Thy Holy Spirit didst preside in the first assembly of the apostles and elders at Jerusalem, and dost still inhabit the whole company of the faithful; mercifully regard, we beseech Thee, Thy servants gathered before Thee at this time, as the chief court and council of this Church. Shed down upon them all heavenly wisdom and grace; enlighten them with true knowledge of Thy

Word; inflame them with a pure zeal for Thy glory; and so order all their doings through Thy good Spirit that unity and peace may prevail among them; that truth and righteousness may flow forth from them; and that, by their endeavours, all Thy ministers and congregations may be established and comforted, Thy Gospel everywhere purely preached and truly followed, Thy kingdom among men extended and strengthened, and the whole body of Thine elect people grow up into Him who is Head over all things to the Church, Jesus Christ our Lord.

Amen.

For Particular Persons: as in Cases of Discipline before the Kirk-Session.

1.

Almighty God, who hast not suffered Thy mercy to be overcome by the greatness of our offences, but turnest Thyself again when Thou hearest the cry of the penitent; look down, we beseech Thee, upon this Thy servant, who confesseth *his* grievous sin, and casteth *himself* upon Thy mercy. It is Thine to wash away our sins, and to vouchsafe Thy pardon to our offences. Thou desirest not the death of a sinner, but rather that he should turn from his wickedness and live. Thou hast declared that there is joy in heaven over one sinner that repenteth. We beseech Thee, therefore, mercifully to forgive Thy servant who acknowledgeth *his* trespasses; receive and comfort *him* who is grieved and wearied with the burden of *his* sins; and grant unto *him*, of Thine infinite goodness, pardon instead of judgment, joy for grief, and life instead of death. Hear us, O most merciful Father, for the sake of Jesus Christ. **Amen.**

2.

O most merciful God, who according to the multitude of Thy mercies dost so put away the sins of those who truly repent, that Thou rememberest them no more; regard with Thine eye of mercy this Thy servant, who hath sought Thy pardon and forgiveness. Renew in *him*, most loving Father, whatsoever hath been decayed or corrupted through *his* own carnal will or frailty, or by the fraud and malice of the devil. Preserve and keep *him* henceforth in the unity of Thy holy Church, and strengthen *him* continually with Thy divine and live-giving Spirit. Restore unto *him* the joy of Thy salvation and the light of Thy countenance, that *he* may abide Thy faithful servant unto everlasting life; through Jesus Christ our Lord, who liveth and reigneth with Thee, O Father, in the unity of the Holy Ghost, one God, world without end. **Amen.**

Thanksgivings.

For Fair Weather.

O Lord God, who hast justly humbled us by Thy late plague of immoderate rain and waters, and in Thy mercy hast relieved and comforted our souls by this seasonable and blessed change of weather; we praise and glorify Thy holy name for this Thy mercy, and will always declare Thy loving-kindness from generation to generation; through Jesus Christ our Lord.
Amen.

In Time of Harvest.

O Lord God Almighty, the fountain of all goodness, by whose word alone all things receive increase and are brought unto perfection, and by whose appointment the fruits of the earth are given for meat unto the children of men; we offer unto Thee our praises and thanksgivings that Thou hast brought us through the circuit of another year, and that, according to Thy promise, seed-time and harvest have not failed. [Thou hast crowned the year with Thy goodness; the earth at Thy commandment hath brought forth abundantly; and our barns are filled with plenty.] We give thanks unto Thy holy name, we rejoice before Thee and praise Thee, for Thy goodness to us and to all the creatures of Thy hand; for Thou art the giver of all good gifts, and unto Thee we render glory and praise, even unto the Father, and unto the Son, and unto the Holy Ghost, now and for evermore, world without end. **Amen.**

For Plenty.

O most merciful Father, who of Thy gracious goodness hast heard the devout prayers of Thy Church, and turned our dearth and scarcity into cheapness and plenty; we give Thee humble thanks for this Thy special bounty; beseeching Thee to continue Thy loving-kindness unto us, that our land may yield us her fruits of increase, to Thy glory and our comfort; through Jesus Christ our Lord. **Amen.**

For Deliverance from Pestilence.

O most merciful Father, who in the midst of Thy judgments hast remembered mercy; we meekly acknowledge Thy marvellous loving-kindness towards us, and Thy tender goodness. Thou didst visit us with Thy sore displeasure; but in Thine abundant mercy Thou hast hearkened unto the prayer of Thy people, and hast assuaged the plague of sickness with which Thou hast lately afflicted us. We render unto Thy divine majesty our humble thanksgivings, and rejoice in Thy salvation. We laud and magnify Thine ever-glorious and honourable name, the name of the Father, and of the Son, and of the Holy Ghost; and unto Thee, in Thy holy Church, we ascribe glory and worship, power and dominion, blessing and praise, now, henceforth, and for evermore, world without end. **Amen.**

For Peace and Deliverance from Enemies.

O Almighty God, who art a strong tower of defence unto Thy servants against the face of their enemies; we yield Thee praise and thanksgiving for our deliverance from those great and apparent dangers wherewith we were compassed. We acknowledge it to be of Thy goodness that we were not delivered over as a prey unto them; beseeching Thee still to continue Thy mercies towards us, that all the world may know that Thou art our Saviour and mighty Deliverer; through Jesus Christ our Lord, who liveth and reigneth with Thee, O Father, in the unity of the Holy Ghost, one God, world without end. **Amen.**

For a Safe Voyage.

Most gracious Lord, whose tender mercy is over all Thy works; we praise Thy holy name, that

Thou hast been pleased to conduct us in safety through the perils of the deep, and to bring us to the end of our journey in peace. May we be duly sensible of Thy merciful providence toward us, and ever express our thankfulness by a holy trust in Thee, and obedience to Thy commandments; through Jesus Christ our Lord.

Amen.

For Deliverance from Storms.

O most merciful and mighty God, who at Thy pleasure raisest the winds and waves of the sea, or commandest them back to peace; we, Thy creatures, spared by Thy mercy to praise Thee, do give Thee unfeigned thanks, for that Thou heardest our cry when we were at the brink of death, and didst not suffer us to perish in the devouring waters. And we here offer ourselves, our bodies and our souls, which Thou hast redeemed, to be a living sacrifice unto Thee of praise and thanksgiving, all the days of our lives; through Jesus Christ our Lord.

Amen.

III.

Prayers for Special Graces.

For Life in Christ.

WE approach Thee, O Lord, in the name of Thy Son Jesus Christ, who, after He had borne our sins and carried our sorrows upon earth, sat down at Thine own right hand, the Mediator of those for whom He died. Grant us, we beseech Thee, to be made partakers, both in that atonement which He perfected on the cross and in His mediation in the upper sanctuary; that, being reconciled through the death of Thy Son, we may be saved by His life, who liveth and was dead, and is alive for evermore, and hath the keys of hell and of death; to whom be glory both now and for ever. Amen.

For Restoration.

O God, who art long-suffering and kind, and art evermore seeking to turn us from our vanities that we may live and not die; grant that we may know this the time of our visitation, and give ear to the voice that calleth us, and so bring us home, good Lord, from wandering in the wilderness, and give our weary hearts such rest in Thee that we may seek to wander from Thee no more, but abide in Thy peace for ever; through Jesus Christ our Lord. **Amen.**

For Conversion to the Will of God.

1.

Almighty and everlasting God, who requirest the hearts of Thy creatures, convert us wholly to Thyself; turn away our eyes from beholding vanity, and quicken us in Thy way; through Him who is at once the pattern and the power of godliness, Thy Son Jesus Christ our Lord. **Amen.**

2.

Almighty God, who hast given Thine only Son to be unto us both a sacrifice for sin and also an ensample of godly life; give us grace that we may always most thankfully receive that His inestimable benefit, and also daily endeavour ourselves to follow the blessed steps of His most holy life; through the same Jesus Christ our Lord. **Amen.**

For Help in Trouble.

1.

O God, the High and Holy One who inhabitest eternity, and dwelleth with him also who is of a contrite and humble spirit, to revive the spirit of the humble and to revive the heart of the contrite ones; glorify Thy grace, we beseech Thee, in the midst of our manifold infirmities and sins, and through all temptation hold us up by Thy mighty hand; that the trial of our faith, being much more precious than of gold that perisheth, though it be tried with fire, may be found unto praise, and honour, and glory, at the appearing of Jesus Christ; to whom, with Thee and the Holy Ghost, be honour and glory, world without end. *Amen.*

2.

Assist us mercifully, O Lord, in these our supplications and prayers, and dispose the way of Thy servants towards the attainment of everlasting salvation; that among all the changes and chances of this mortal life, they may ever be defended by Thy most gracious and ready help, through Jesus Christ our Lord. *Amen.*

For Grace.

1.

O Lord God, strong to deliver, and mighty to save, who hast been the refuge and dwelling-place of Thy people in all generations, perfect and fulfil in us, we beseech Thee, the work of Thy converting grace, and be pleased to confirm in us every good purpose and deed; that having been called into the way of righteousness, we may have power to continue steadfastly in the same, until the day of Jesus Christ; to whom, with Thee and the Holy Ghost, be all honour and praise, world without end. **Amen.**

2.

Almighty and eternal God, who dost bid us walk as pilgrims and strangers in this passing world, seeking that abiding city which Thou hast prepared for us in heaven; we pray Thee so to govern our hearts by Thy Holy Spirit, that we, avoiding all fleshly lusts which war against the soul, and quietly obedient to the rule which Thou hast set over us, may show forth Thy glory before the world by our good works; for Jesus Christ's sake. **Amen.**

3.

O God, the strength of all them that put their trust in Thee, mercifully accept our prayers; and because, through the weakness of our mortal nature, we can do no good thing without Thee, grant us the help of Thy grace, that in keeping of Thy commandments we may please Thee both in will and in deed; through Jesus Christ our Lord. **Amen.**

For Peace.

1.

O God, from whom all holy desires, all good counsels, and all just works, do proceed; give unto Thy servants that peace which the world cannot give; that both our hearts may be set to obey Thy commandments, and also that by Thee we, being defended from the fear of our enemies, may pass our time in rest and quietness; through the merits of Jesus Christ our Saviour. **Amen.**

2.

O God, who art the author of peace and lover of concord, in knowledge of whom standeth our eternal life, whose service is perfect freedom: defend us Thy humble servants in all assaults of our enemies; that we, surely trusting in Thy defence, may not fear the power of any adversary, through the might of Jesus Christ our Lord. **Amen.**

For Heavenly-Mindedness.

1.

O Almighty God, who alone canst order the unruly wills and affections of sinful men; grant unto Thy people that they may love the thing which Thou commandest, and desire that which Thou dost promise; that so, among the sundry and manifold changes of the world, our hearts may surely there be fixed, where true joys are to be found; through Jesus Christ our Lord.
Amen.

2.

Almighty God, the former of our bodies and Father of our spirits, in whom we live, move, and have our being; shed abroad Thy love in our hearts, we beseech Thee, and cause the comfort of Thy heavenly grace to abound in us, as the earnest and pledge of joys to come; that, casting away all anxious thought for the transitory things of this world, we may seek first Thy kingdom and righteousness, and labour only for that meat which endureth unto everlasting life; through Jesus Christ our Lord. *Amen.*

3.

O God, whose favour is life, and in whose presence there is fulness of peace and joy;

vouchsafe unto us, we beseech Thee, such an abiding sense of the reality and glory of those things which Thou hast prepared for them that love Thee, as may serve to raise us above the vanity of this present world, both in its pleasures and in its necessary trials and pains; so that under Thy guidance and help all things here shall work together for our everlasting salvation; through Jesus Christ our Lord.

Amen.

4.

Blessed be Thou, O God and Father of our Lord Jesus Christ, who, according to Thine abundant mercy, hast begotten us again to a lively hope by the resurrection of Jesus Christ from the dead, to an inheritance incorruptible, and undefiled, and that fadeth not away, reserved for us in heaven. Grant, we beseech Thee, that having this hope in us, we may be led by Thy grace to walk worthy of it. May we be crucified unto the world, and raised with Christ to newness of life. As risen with Him, enable us also in heart and mind to ascend with Him to heavenly places, and to seek those things which are above, where He sitteth at Thy right hand. And grant that, having our conversation in heaven, and our life hid with Christ in God, we may rest in the confident persuasion that when He who is our life shall appear, we also shall appear with Him in glory; to whom, with Thee and the Holy Ghost, be glory for ever. **Amen.**

For Purity.

1.

O God, whose blessed Son was manifested that He might destroy the works of the devil, and make us the sons of God and heirs of eternal life, grant us, we beseech Thee, that, having this hope, we may purify ourselves, even as He is pure; that when He shall appear again with power and great glory, we may be made like unto Him in His eternal and glorious kingdom: where with Thee, O Father, and Thee, O Holy Ghost, He liveth and reigneth, ever one God, world without end. **Amen.**

2.

Almighty God, our most holy and eternal Father, who art of purer eyes than to behold evil, let Thy gracious and Holy Spirit descend upon Thy servants; that no impure thoughts may pollute that soul which Thou hast sanctified, no impure words pollute that tongue which Thou hast ordained an organ of Thy praise, no impure action rend the veil of that temple which Thou hast chosen for an habitation; but grant that, our senses being sealed up from all vain objects, our hearts entirely possessed with religion, and fortified with prudence, watchfulness, and self-denial, we may so live in this present world as not to fail of the glories of the world to come.

Amen.

For Guidance.

1.

O Thou great Shepherd of Israel, who, by Thine outstretched arm, didst bring Thy people of old out of the land of Egypt and the house of bondage, guiding them safely through the wilderness to the promised land; we pray Thee to deliver us from the bondage and slavery of our sins, and so to lead us through the wilderness of this world, feeding us with bread from heaven, and with water out of the smitten Rock, and upholding us amid the swellings of Jordan, that we may enter at last into that rest which remaineth for Thy faithful people. *Amen.*

2.

O God, the Protector of all that trust in Thee, without whom nothing is strong, nothing is holy; increase and multiply upon us Thy mercy, that Thou being our ruler and guide, we may so pass through things temporal, that we finally lose not the things eternal. Grant this, O heavenly Father, for Jesus Christ's sake, our Lord.

Amen.

For Faith.

O Almighty and everlasting God, who not only givest every good and perfect gift, but also increasest those gifts Thou hast bestowed; we most humbly beseech Thee to increase in us the gift of faith, that we may truly believe in Thee and in Thy promises; and that neither by our negligence, nor infirmity of the flesh, nor by grievousness of temptation, nor by the subtle crafts and assaults of the devil, we may be driven from faith in our most blessed Lord and Saviour Jesus Christ; to whom, with Thee and the Holy Ghost, be glory for ever. **Amen.**

For Hope.

O God, under whose wise and righteous order the whole creation groaneth and travaileth in pain together until now, as having been made subject to vanity by reason of sin; graciously help the infirmities of Thy people, we humbly beseech Thee, and raise them up through the strong power of Christian hope; that we also, who have received the first-fruits of the Spirit, may not seek our rest in this mortal state, but inwardly long after that which is far better, to be with Christ in heaven; to whom, with Thee and the Holy Ghost, be honour and glory, world without end. **Amen.**

For Love.

1.

O God, who hast taught Thy Church to keep all Thy heavenly commandments by loving Thee and our neighbour; grant us the spirit of peace and grace, that Thy universal family may be both devoted to Thee with their whole heart, and united to each other with a pure will; through Jesus Christ our Lord. **Amen.**

2.

O God, who hast prepared for them that love Thee such good things as pass man's understanding; pour into our hearts such love towards Thee, that we, loving Thee above all things, may obtain Thy promises, which exceed all that we can desire; through Jesus Christ our Lord. **Amen.**

3.

O God, the strength of all them that put their trust in Thee, who hast not appointed us unto wrath, but to obtain salvation by our Lord Jesus Christ; because through the weakness of our mortal nature we can do no good thing without Thee, we beseech Thee to grant us the help of Thy grace, and to breathe into us that divine charity which is the fulfilling of the law;

that in keeping of Thy commandments we may please Thee both in will and in deed, and be counted worthy, after the sufferings of this life, to reign with Christ in heaven; to whom, with Thee and the Holy Ghost, be honour and glory, world without end. **Amen.**

4.

O Lord, who hast taught us that all our doings without charity are nothing worth, send Thy Holy Ghost, and pour into our hearts that most excellent gift of charity, the very bond of peace, and of all virtues, without which whosoever liveth is counted dead before Thee: grant this for Thine only Son Jesus Christ's sake.

Amen.

For Fortitude.

Almighty and most merciful God, whose name is a strong tower into which the righteous runneth and is safe; lift up the standard of Thy Spirit, we beseech Thee, against the power of the enemy coming in upon us like a flood, and clothe us with the full armour of righteousness on the right hand and on the left, that we may be able to fight manfully the good fight of faith, and so finish our course with joy in the great day when Christ, the righteous Judge, shall

appear; who liveth and reigneth with Thee in the unity of the Holy Ghost, ever one God.
Amen.

For Patience.

1.

O God, who didst will Thine only-begotten Son to learn obedience by the things which He suffered, that being thus made perfect He might become the Author of eternal salvation unto all them that obey Him; work in us, we beseech Thee, such inward conformity with His holy patience, as may cause us to have part also in His glorious power; that so, walking not after the flesh but after the Spirit, we may be able to serve Thee all our days in newness of mind and life; through Jesus Christ our Lord.
Amen.

2.

Almighty and everlasting God, the Creator of the ends of the earth, who givest power to the faint, and strength to them that have no might; look mercifully, we beseech Thee, on our low estate, and cause Thy grace to triumph in our weakness, that we may arise and follow in the way of righteousness those who by their faith and patience already inherit the promises; through Jesus Christ our Lord. *Amen.*

For Cheerfulness.

O most loving Father, who willest us to give thanks for all things, to dread nothing but the loss of Thee, and to cast all our cares on Thee who carest for us; preserve us from faithless fears and worldly anxieties, and grant that no clouds of this mortal life may hide from us the light of that love which is immortal, and which Thou hast manifested to us in Thy Son Jesus Christ our Lord. Amen.

For Temperance.

Almighty God, gracious Father of men and angels, who openest Thine hand and fillest all things with plenty; teach us to use the gifts of Thy providence soberly and temperately, that our temptations may not be too strong for us, our bodies healthless, or our affections sensual and unholy. Grant, O Lord, that the blessings which Thou givest us may neither minister to sin nor to sickness, but to health and holiness and thanksgiving; that in the strength of Thy provision we may faithfully and diligently serve Thee, may worthily feast at Thy table here, and be accounted worthy to sit down at Thy table hereafter; through Jesus Christ our Lord. Amen.

For Protection.

1.

O God, who knowest us to be set in the midst of so many and great dangers, that by reason of the frailty of our nature we cannot always stand upright; grant to us such strength and protection as may support us in all dangers, and carry us through all temptations; through Jesus Christ our Lord. Amen.

2.

Almighty God, who seest that we have no power of ourselves to help ourselves, keep us both outwardly in our bodies and inwardly in our souls, that we may be defended from all adversities which may happen to the body, and from all evil thoughts which may assault and hurt the soul; through Jesus Christ our Lord.

Amen.

3.

O Almighty Lord and everlasting God, vouchsafe, we beseech Thee, to direct, sanctify, and govern both our hearts and bodies in the ways of Thy laws, and in the works of Thy commandments; that through Thy most mighty protection, both here and ever, we may be preserved in body and soul, through our Lord and Saviour Jesus Christ. Amen.

For Temporal and Spiritual Blessings.

O God, who knowest that while we are in this life we have manifold bodily wants to be supplied, and hast graciously promised to them that seek first Thy kingdom and righteousness that all other needful things shall be added to them; grant us such a competent portion of earthly blessings as Thy wisdom seeth to be suitable and expedient for us. We ask of Thee neither poverty nor riches, but food to eat and raiment to put on. Give to us skill and industry to provide for ourselves and those who are dependent on us; and bless us in all the works of our hands, that we may have sufficient not to be chargeable, but rather to be helpful, to others. Suffer us not in prosperity to forget, or in adversity to think ourselves forgotten of, Thee. Above all, grant that our spiritual wants may be more and more abundantly supplied through the fulness of the blessings of Thy Gospel, to the end that, growing in knowledge and in grace, our souls may be strengthened and nourished unto life eternal; through Jesus Christ our Lord. **Amen.**

For Edification.

O Almighty God, who hast begotten us through Thy Word, renewed us by Thy Spirit, nourished us by Thy sacraments and by the ministry of Thy Church, be pleased still to build us up to life eternal. Give us understanding in Thy law, that we may know Thy will, and grace and strength faithfully to fulfil the same. Grant that our understandings may know Thee, our hearts may love Thee, and all our faculties and powers give Thee due obedience and service; so that, escaping from the darkness of this world, we may at length come to the land of everlasting rest, in Thy light to behold light and glory; through Jesus Christ our Lord. Amen.

For Grace to Redeem the Time.

O God, who hast made our days as an handbreadth, so that our age is as nothing before Thee; impress us with a sense of our frailty, and so teach us to number our days that we may apply our hearts unto wisdom. Dispose us to walk circumspectly, redeeming the time; to be sober, watchful, and prayerful; and to do with all our might whatsoever our hand findeth, for the advancement of Thy glory, the good of our fellow-men, and the furtherance of our own spiritual welfare; and grant that after having done and suffered Thy will upon the earth, we may have an entrance ministered to us abundantly into the everlasting kingdom of our Lord and Saviour Jesus Christ; to whom, with Thee and the Holy Ghost, be glory for ever. **Amen.**

Against Spiritual Apathy.

O God, the sovereign good of the soul, who requirest the hearts of all Thy children; deliver us from all sloth in Thy work, all coldness in Thy cause; and grant that by looking unto Thee we may rekindle our love, and by waiting upon Thee may renew our strength; through Jesus Christ our Lord. **Amen.**

IV.

Collects and Prayers for Natural and Sacred Seasons.

The Advent of our Lord.

1.

ALMIGHTY GOD, we beseech Thee, grant unto Thy people grace that they may wait with vigilance for the advent of Thy Son our Lord, that when He shall arise from Thy right hand to visit the earth in righteousness and Thy people with salvation, He may not find us sleeping in sin, but diligent in Thy service, and rejoicing in Thy praises, that so we may enter in with Him unto the marriage of the Lamb; through His merits, who liveth and reigneth with Thee and the Holy Ghost, ever one God, world without end. **Amen.**

2.

God of all grace and comfort, who hast not appointed us unto wrath, but to obtain salvation by our Lord Jesus Christ; aid us, we beseech Thee, at this time, to repent heartily and truly of all our sins, and so to humble ourselves that when He cometh we may be prepared to receive Him with childlike faith, and join in the glad cry, Hosanna to the Son of David! Blessed is He that cometh in the name of the Lord!
Amen.

3.

Almighty God, give us grace that we may cast away the works of darkness, and put upon us the armour of light, now in the time of this mortal life, in which Thy Son Jesus Christ came to visit us in great humility, that in the last day, when He shall come again in His glorious majesty to judge both the quick and the dead, we may rise to the life immortal; through Him who liveth and reigneth with Thee and the Holy Ghost, now and ever. **Amen.**

4.

O Lord Jesus Christ, who at Thy first coming didst send Thy messenger to prepare the way before Thee, grant that the ministers and stewards of Thy mysteries may likewise so prepare and make ready Thy way, by turning the hearts of the disobedient to the wisdom of the just, that at Thy second coming to judge the world, we may be found an acceptable people in Thy sight, who livest and reignest with the Father and the Holy Ghost, ever one God, world without end. **Amen.**

5.

O Almighty God, grant that those necessary works wherein we are engaged, whether in the affairs of Thy Church or of this world, may not prevail to hinder us; but that, at the appearing and advent of Thy Son, we may hasten with joy to meet Him, who liveth and reigneth with Thee and the Holy Ghost, ever one God, world without end. **Amen.**

6.

O Lord, raise up, we pray Thee, Thy power, and come among us, and with great might succour us; that whereas, through our sins and wickedness, we are sore let and hindered in running the race that is set before us, Thy bountiful grace and mercy may speedily help and deliver us; through Thy Son our Lord, to whom with Thee and the Holy Ghost be honour and glory, world without end. **Amen.**

The Incarnation of our Lord.

1.

Most merciful God, who hast so loved the world as to give Thine only-begotten Son, that whosoever believeth in Him should not perish but have everlasting life; vouchsafe unto us, we humbly pray Thee, the precious gift of faith, whereby we may know that the Son of God is come; and, being always rooted and grounded in the mystery of the Word made flesh, may have power to overcome the world, and gain the blessed immortality of heaven; through the merits of the same incarnate Christ, who liveth and reigneth with Thee in the unity of the Holy Ghost, ever one God, world without end.

Amen.

2.

Almighty and everlasting God, who hast given us Thy only-begotten Son to take our nature upon Him, and as at this time to be born of a pure virgin; grant that we, being regenerate and made Thy children by adoption and grace, may daily be renewed by Thy Holy Spirit after the image of this same blessed and glorious Christ; who liveth and reigneth with Thee and the Holy Ghost, ever one God, world without end.

Amen.

3.

O Almighty God, who by the birth of Thy Holy One into the world didst give Thy true light to dawn upon our darkness; grant that as Thou hast given us to believe in the mystery of His incarnation, and hast made us partakers of the divine nature, so in the world to come we may ever abide with Him, in the glory of His kingdom; through the same Jesus Christ our Lord. **Amen.**

4.

O God, who makest us glad with the yearly remembrance of the birth of Thine only Son Jesus Christ; grant that as we joyfully receive Him for our Redeemer, so we may with sure confidence behold Him when He shall come to be our Judge; who liveth and reigneth with Thee and the Holy Ghost, one God, world without end. **Amen.**

At the Beginning of the Year.

Almighty and eternal God, with whom one day is as a thousand years, and a thousand years as one day; we bring Thee thanks and praise for Thy blessings, more than we can number, with which Thou hast crowned our lives during the year now past; and, since Thy mercies are ever new, let the year which has now begun be to us a year of grace and salvation. Have pity upon us in our misery, whose days are as the grass; deliver us from the vanity of our fallen nature, and establish us in the fellowship of that life which is the same yesterday, and to-day, and for ever. Graciously protect and conduct us through the uncertainties of this new year of our earthly pilgrimage; prepare us for its duties and trials, its joys and sorrows; help us to watch and pray, and to be always ready like men that wait for their Lord; and grant that every change, whether it be of prosperity or adversity, of life or death, may bring us nearer to Thee, and to that great eternal year of joy and rest, which, after the years of this vain earthly life, awaits the faithful in Thy blissful presence; when we shall unite with angels and saints in ascribing blessing, and honour, and glory, and power, unto Him who sitteth upon the throne, and unto the Lamb, for ever and ever. Amen.

The Circumcision of our Lord.

Almighty God, who madest Thy blessed Son to be circumcised, and obedient to the law for man; grant us the true circumcision of the Spirit, that our hearts and all our members being mortified from all worldly and carnal lusts, we may in all things obey Thy blessed will; through the same Thy Son Jesus Christ our Lord. Amen.

The Manifestation of our Lord to the Gentiles.

O God, who by the leading of a star didst manifest Thy only-begotten Son to the Gentiles; mercifully grant that we who know Thee now by faith, may after this life have the fruition of Thy glorious Godhead; through Jesus Christ our Lord. **Amen.**

Palm Sunday.

1.

O Lord Jesus Christ, who as on this day didst enter the rebellious city where Thou wast to die; enter into our hearts, we beseech Thee, and subdue them wholly to Thyself. And as Thy faithful disciples blessed Thy coming, and spread their garments in the way, covering it with palm branches, may we be ready to lay at Thy feet all that we have and are, and to bless Thee, O Thou who comest in the name of the Lord. And grant that after having confessed and worshipped Thee upon the earth, we may be among the number of those who shall hail Thine eternal triumphs, and bear in their hands the palms of victory, when every knee shall bow before Thee, and every tongue confess that Thou art Lord, and that Thou shalt reign for ever and ever. **Amen.**

238 COLLECTS AND PRAYERS.

2.

Almighty and everlasting God, who of Thy tender mercy towards mankind hast sent Thy Son, our Saviour Jesus Christ, to take upon Him our flesh and to suffer death upon the cross, that all mankind should follow the example of His great humility; mercifully grant that we may both follow the example of His patience, and also be made partakers of His resurrection; through the same Jesus Christ our Lord.
Amen.

The Passion and Crucifixion of our Lord.

1.

Almighty God, we beseech Thee graciously to behold this Thy family, for which our Lord Jesus Christ was contented to be betrayed, and given up into the hands of wicked men, and to suffer death upon the cross; who now liveth and reigneth with Thee and the Holy Ghost, ever one God, world without end. **Amen.**

2.

O most merciful Father, who of Thy tender compassion towards us guilty sinners didst give Thine only-begotten Son to be an offering for our sins; grant us grace, we humbly beseech Thee, that, being united unto Him by Thy Spirit,

and made partakers of His sufferings and His death, we may crucify the corrupt inclinations of the flesh, die daily unto the world, and lead holy and unblamable lives. Cleaving unto His cross in all the temptations of life, may we hold fast the profession of our faith without wavering, and finally attain unto the resurrection of the just; through the merits of this same once crucified but now risen and exalted Saviour.
Amen.

3.

Lord Jesus Christ, Thou holy and spotless Lamb of God, who didst take upon Thyself the curse of sin which was due to us; we unite with all the heavenly host of the redeemed in ascribing unto Thee power, and riches, and wisdom, and strength, and honour, and glory, and blessing. We bless Thee for all the burdens Thou hast borne, for all the tears Thou hast wept, for all the pains Thou hast suffered, for every word of comfort Thou hast spoken on the cross, for every conflict with the powers of darkness, and for Thine eternal victory over the terrors of death and the pains of hell. **Amen.**

The Burial of our Lord.

1.

O Almighty God, who by the descent of our Saviour Jesus Christ into hell, and His rising again from the dead, hast given assurance that the spirits of those who sleep in Him do abide in joy and felicity; grant unto us, we beseech Thee, such steadfast faith and lively hope, that we may purify ourselves as He is pure; and that we, with Thy whole redeemed Church, may speedily attain unto the resurrection from the dead, when our mortal bodies shall put on immortality and incorruption, and we shall be changed into the likeness of His glorious body; who liveth and abideth with Thee and the Holy Ghost, one God, world without end. Amen.

2.

Grant, O Lord, that as we are baptized into the death of Thy blessed Son our Saviour Jesus Christ, so, by continual mortifying our corrupt affections, we may be buried with Him; and that through the grave and gate of death we may pass to our joyful resurrection, for His merits, who died and was buried, and rose again for us, Thy Son Jesus Christ our Lord. Amen.

The Resurrection of our Lord.

1.

Almighty God, who through Thine only-begotten Son Jesus Christ hast overcome death, and opened unto us the gates of everlasting life;

we humbly beseech Thee that as, by Thy special grace preventing us, Thou dost put into our minds good desires, so by Thy continual help we may bring the same to good effect; through Jesus Christ our Lord, who liveth and reigneth with Thee and the Holy Ghost, ever one God, world without end. Amen.

2.

Almighty God, who hast brought again from the dead our Lord Jesus, the glorious Prince of salvation, with everlasting victory over hell and the grave; grant us power, we beseech Thee, to rise with Him to newness of life, that we may overcome the world with the victory of faith, and have part at last in the resurrection of the just; through the merits of the same risen Saviour, who liveth and reigneth with Thee and the Holy Ghost, ever one God, world without end. Amen.

3.

O Thou God and Father of our Lord Jesus Christ, we render Thee most humble and hearty thanks that when He had descended into the grave, Thou didst not suffer Thy Holy One to see corruption, but didst show unto Him the path of life and raise Him from the dead, and set Him at Thine own right hand in the heavenly places. Grant us grace, we beseech Thee, to apprehend with true faith the glorious mystery of our Saviour's resurrection, and fill our hearts with joy, and a lively hope that amid all the sorrows, trials, and temptations of our mortal state, and in the hour of death, we may derive strength and comfort from this sure pledge of an inheritance incorruptible and undefiled, and that fadeth not away. **Amen.**

4.

Almighty God, Father of our Lord Jesus Christ, who didst raise up Thy Son from the dead and give Him glory, that our faith and hope might be in Thee; quicken us also, we beseech Thee, by Thy mighty power, from the death of sin to the life of righteousness, and cause us to set our affections on things above; so that we may, at the last day, have part in the resurrection of the just, and in the glory of Thy heavenly kingdom, whither Jesus the forerunner is for us entered, where also He liveth and reigneth with Thee and the Holy Ghost, God blessed for ever. **Amen.**

5.

O Thou, Prince of life and first-begotten of the dead, whom not having seen we love; breathe upon us that we may receive the Holy Ghost, to abide with us continually, both as the seal of our adoption, and as an earnest of the promised possession. Give us power to walk in the Spirit that we may not fulfil the lusts of the flesh, but mortify our members which are upon the earth, and purify ourselves even as Thou art pure, so that at Thy second coming to judge the world in righteousness, we also may appear with Thee, having our vile bodies changed into the fashion of Thine own glorious body, according to the working whereby Thou art able even to subdue all things unto Thyself, who art God over all, blessed for ever. Amen.

The Ascension of our Lord.

1.

O Lord Jesus Christ, Thou Conqueror of death and hell, who from the depths of Thy humiliation didst pass into the heavens, and art crowned with glory and honour as King of saints and eternal High Priest over the house of God; let Thy all-powerful intercessions prevail on our behalf, that, being delivered from the curse of sin, we may receive grace and strength to follow Thee with patient endurance through the sorrows and pains of earth, and the darkness of the grave, and having thus shared in Thy sufferings here, become partaker also of Thy joy and glory in the everlasting kingdom of the Father.
Amen.

2.

Grant, we beseech Thee, Almighty God, that like as we do believe Thine only-begotten Son, our Lord Jesus Christ, to have ascended into the heavens; so we may also in heart and mind thither ascend, and with Him continually dwell, who liveth and reigneth with Thee and the Holy Ghost, one God, world without end. **Amen.**

3.

O God, the King of glory, who hast exalted Thine only Son Jesus Christ with great triumph into Thy kingdom in heaven; we beseech Thee, leave us not comfortless; but send to us Thy Holy Ghost to comfort us, and exalt us unto the same place whither our Saviour Christ has gone before; who liveth and reigneth with Thee and the Holy Ghost, one God, world without end

Amen.

The Descent of the Holy Ghost.

1.

God of all peace and consolation, who didst gloriously fulfil the great promise of the Gospel by sending down the Holy Ghost on the day of Pentecost, to establish the Church as the house of His continual presence and power among men; mercifully grant unto us, we beseech Thee, this same gift of the Spirit, to renew, illuminate, refresh, and sanctify our souls; to be over us and around us like the light and dew of heaven, and to be in us evermore as a well of water springing up into everlasting life; through Jesus Christ our Lord. **Amen.**

2.

Most glorious and blessed God, who through the Holy Ghost hast made Thy one Catholic Church to be the body of Christ, the fulness of Him that filleth all in all; we humbly beseech Thee to grant unto us, and to all Thy people, such strong and steadfast faith in this great mystery of grace, that, being safely defended from all heresy and schism, we may ever abide in the unity of the Spirit, and so grow up into Him in all things, which is the Head, even Christ: to whom, with Thee and the Holy Ghost ever one God, be all honour and praise, world without end. **Amen.**

3.

O Almighty God, who hast sent down the Holy Ghost upon Thine elect, endowing them with His manifold gifts, and knitting them together in one communion and fellowship in the mystical body of Thy Son; grant unto us grace to use all those Thy gifts alway to Thy honour and glory, and to abound in faith, hope, and charity, waiting for Thy Son from heaven; that when He shall appear, we with all Thy saints may be found of Him in peace, and by Him may be presented before Thy glorious presence with exceeding joy; through the same Jesus Christ our Lord, who liveth and reigneth with Thee, O Father, in the unity of the same Holy Ghost, ever one God, world without end.

Amen.

4.

O Holy Ghost, Spirit of the Father and the Son, who by Thy quickening energy hast raised us up to a new life in Christ Jesus, and dost in mercy to our infirmities condescend to dwell in our mortal bodies as Thy consecrated temples; bring forth in our hearts and lives, we beseech Thee, the fruits of love, joy, peace, long-suffering, gentleness, faith, meekness, and temperance; that so walking in Thee with all holy obedience, we may stand firm in the knowledge and love of the truth, against the wiles of the devil, may overcome the world, and be glorified in the fellowship of the Father and the Son; to whom, with Thee, who art coequal and coeternal God, we ascribe all honour, thanksgiving, and praise.

Amen.

5.

O God, who at this time didst teach the hearts of Thy faithful people, by the sending to them the light of Thy Holy Spirit; grant us by the same Spirit to have a right judgment in all things, and evermore to rejoice in His holy comfort; through the merits of Christ Jesus our Saviour, who liveth and reigneth with Thee, in the unity of the same Spirit, one God, world without end. Amen.

The Holy Trinity.

Almighty and everlasting God, who hast given unto us Thy servants grace, by the confession of a true faith to acknowledge the glory of the eternal Trinity, and in the power of the divine Majesty to worship the Unity; we beseech Thee that Thou wouldst keep us steadfast in this faith, and evermore defend us from all adversities; who livest and reignest one God, world without end. Amen.

All Angels.

O everlasting God, who hast ordained and constituted the services of Angels and men in a wonderful order; mercifully grant, that as Thy holy Angels alway do Thee service in heaven, so by Thy appointment they may succour and defend us on earth; through Jesus Christ our Lord. Amen.

Communion of Saints.

1.

O God, the Father everlasting, whom the glorious hosts of heaven obey, and in whose presence patriarchs, prophets, apostles, martyrs, with all the spirits of the just made perfect, continually do live; fix the eye of our faith, we beseech Thee, with clear and full vision, on the great cloud of witnesses wherewith we are compassed about, that laying aside every weight, and the sin that doth so easily beset us, we may run with patience the race that is set before us, and obtain at last the crown of everlasting life; through Jesus Christ our Lord. Amen.

2.

O Almighty God, who hast knit together Thine elect in one communion and fellowship, in the mystical Body of Thy Son Christ our Lord; grant us grace so to follow Thy blessed saints in all virtuous and godly living, that we may come to those unspeakable joys which Thou hast prepared for them that unfeignedly love Thee; through Jesus Christ our Lord. Amen.

V.

Additional Forms of Service.

The following additional Forms may be used at the discretion of the Minister.

Introductory Sentences.

When there is to be Holy Communion.

1.

WHAT shall I render unto the Lord for all His benefits toward me? I will take the cup of salvation, and call upon the name of the Lord. I will offer to Thee the sacrifice of thanksgiving. I will pay my vows unto the Lord now in the presence of all His people.

2.

I will wash mine hands in innocency: so will I compass thine altar, O Lord; that I may publish with the voice of thanksgiving, and tell of all Thy wondrous works.

Lord, I have loved the habitation of Thy house, and the place where Thine honour dwelleth.

O taste and see that the Lord is good: blessed is the man that trusteth in Him.

3.

Who shall ascend into the hill of the Lord? and who shall stand in His holy place? He that hath clean hands, and a pure heart; who hath not lifted up his soul unto vanity, nor sworn deceitfully. He shall receive the blessing from the Lord, and righteousness from the God of his salvation.

4.

If thou bring thy gift to the altar, and there rememberest that thy brother hath ought against thee; leave there thy gift before the altar, and go thy way; first be reconciled to thy brother, and then come and offer thy gift.

5.

Jesus said, I am the Bread of Life: he that cometh to Me shall never hunger; and he that believeth on Me shall never thirst.

Him that cometh unto Me I will in no wise cast out.

6.

Christ our Passover is sacrificed for us; therefore let us keep the feast, not with old leaven, neither with the leaven of malice and wickedness; but with the unleavened bread of sincerity and truth.

Morning.

1.

Let Israel hope in the Lord: for with the Lord there is mercy, and with Him is plenteous redemption.

My voice shalt Thou hear in the morning, O Lord; in the morning will I direct my prayer unto Thee, and will look up.

2.

Thus saith the Lord unto the house of Israel, Seek ye Me, and ye shall live.

Then shall we know, if we follow on to know the Lord: His going forth is prepared as the morning; and He shall come unto us as the rain, as the latter and former rain unto the earth.

3.

Praise waiteth for Thee, O God, in Zion: and unto Thee shall the vow be performed.

O Thou that hearest prayer, unto Thee shall all flesh come.

Whom have I in heaven but Thee? and there is none upon earth that I desire besides Thee.

My flesh and my heart faileth: but God is the strength of my heart, and my portion for ever.

4.

We will come into Thy house in the multitude of Thy mercy; and in Thy fear will we worship toward Thy holy temple.

Let the words of our mouth, and the meditation of our heart, be acceptable in Thy sight, O Lord, our strength and our Redeemer.

Evening.

1.

Except the Lord build the house, they labour in vain that build it: except the Lord keep the city, the watchman waketh but in vain.

I will say of the Lord, He is my refuge, and my fortress: my God; in Him will I trust.

2.

Lord, I cry unto Thee: make haste unto me; give ear unto my voice, when I cry unto Thee.

Let my prayer be set forth before Thee as incense, and the lifting up of my hands as the evening sacrifice.

3.

Come now, and let us reason together, saith the Lord: Though your sins be as scarlet, they shall be as white as snow; though they be red like crimson, they shall be as wool.

I acknowledged my sin unto Thee, and mine iniquity have I not hid. I said, I will confess my transgressions unto the Lord; and Thou forgavest the inquity of my sin.

4.

Wherewith shall I come before the Lord, and bow myself before the high God?

He hath showed thee, O man, what is good; and

what doth the Lord require of thee, but to do justly, and to love mercy, and to walk humbly with thy God?

Prayers of Invocation.

1.

Almighty God, who hast promised to be present with Thy people, and to grant their requests in the name of Thy well-beloved Son; regard us, we humbly beseech Thee, with Thy favour; and for the sake of Him who is our only Saviour and Mediator with Thee, fulfil Thy promise in our behalf, that our thoughts being lifted up, and our desires drawn forth unto Thee, we may render Thee acceptable worship; through Jesus Christ our Lord. **Amen.**

2.

O God, whom heaven and the heaven of heavens cannot contain, but who dwellest with humble and contrite hearts; look in Thy mercy upon us who are here assembled according to Thine ordinance to offer up our sacrifices of prayer and praise before Thy divine majesty. Grant us Thy Holy Spirit, we entreat Thee, O Lord, to guide and to sanctify us, that we may be acceptable in Thy sight, and may obtain our petitions; for we come before Thee not in our own name, but in the name of our great High Priest and Advocate, Jesus Christ. **Amen.**

3.

Almighty God, our heavenly Father, who hast promised to hear us when we call upon Thee in the name of Thy Son, we beseech Thee to regard us in Thy mercy, as we are here assembled to offer unto Thee our praises and our prayers, and to hear Thy Word; and so to raise our thoughts and desires to Thyself, that we may render to Thee an acceptable service; through Jesus Christ our Lord. **Amen.**

4.

O God, the Judge of all, who knowest what is in man, and requirest truth in the inward parts; mercifully grant that we may not draw near to Thee with our lips while our heart is far from Thee; and let Thy Holy Spirit help our infirmities, and pray with us and plead for us, that our offerings may be holy and well-pleasing unto Thee; through the merits of our only Saviour, Jesus Christ our Lord. **Amen.**

5.

Almighty and everlasting God, who lovest the gates of Zion more than all the dwellings of Jacob, and who hast promised that in all places where Thou dost record Thy name, Thou wilt meet with Thy people to bless them; fulfil to us, we beseech Thee, Thy promise, and make us joyful in the house of prayer.

Let our sacrifices of praise and prayer go up with acceptance before Thy throne, through Him who is the great High Priest of our profession, and who has consecrated for us a new and living way into the holiest, that coming boldly to the throne of grace we may obtain mercy, and find grace to help in time of need. Amen.

6.

Almighty and everlasting God, who art always more ready to hear than we to pray, and art wont to give more than either we desire or deserve; pour down upon us the abundance of Thy mercy; forgiving us those things whereof our conscience is afraid, and giving us those good things which we are not worthy to ask but through the merits and mediation of Jesus Christ Thy Son, our Lord. Amen.

7.

O Thou who art greatly to be feared in the assembly of the saints, and to be had in reverence of all them that are round about Thee; be present with us this day, and with all Thy people who worship in Thy holy place. Fill our hearts with Thy fear, and open Thou our lips to make confession and supplication, and to show forth all Thy praise; through Jesus Christ our Lord. Amen.

8.

O Lord our God, great, eternal, wonderful in Thy glory; who keepest covenant and promises for those that love Thee with their whole heart; who art the Life of all, the Help of those that flee unto Thee, the Hope of those who cry unto Thee,—cleanse us from our sins, secret and open, and from every thought displeasing to Thy goodness; cleanse our hearts and consciences, that with a peaceful soul and quiet mind, with perfect love and calm hope, we may venture with confidence and without fear to pray unto Thee; through Jesus Christ our Lord.

Amen.

9.

O most merciful God, who by Thy holy prophet didst foretell that Thy name should be great among the Gentiles, and that in every place incense and a pure offering should be offered unto Thy name; who hast taught us by Thy well-beloved Son, that the hour is come wherein the true worshippers must worship Thee, in every place, in spirit and in truth; grant, we beseech Thee, that we may continually offer unto Thee pure sacrifices, and true and reasonable worship in the Holy Ghost, and may never wander from Thy most·blessed truth, even from the true Shepherd, Jesus Christ our Lord, who liveth and reigneth with Thee, in the unity of the Holy Ghost, one God, world without end. *Amen.*

Confessions.

1.

Give ear, O Lord, unto our prayer, and hearken to our supplications; for we acknowledge our iniquities, and lay bare our sins before Thee. Against Thee, O Lord, have we sinned; to Thee do we make our confession, and implore forgiveness. Turn Thy face,

O Lord, upon Thy servants, whom Thou hast redeemed with the most precious blood of Thy dear Son. Spare us, we beseech Thee; pardon our offences; and be pleased to extend to us Thy lovingkindness and mercy; through Jesus Christ our Lord.
Amen.

2.

Almighty God, Father of our Lord Jesus Christ, Maker of all things, Judge of all men; we cast ourselves down at Thy feet with deep humiliation, in view of our manifold sins and great unrighteousness, whereby we have provoked against ourselves most justly Thine indignation and wrath.

We have sinned against Thee in thought, word, and deed; we have broken Thy holy laws; we have come short of Thy righteousness and glory in all our ways; our lives bear testimony against us, and our own hearts condemn us as being prone to all evil and backward to all good.

We have abused Thy mercies and made light of Thy judgments; we have turned aside from Thy covenant; and we have not been faithful and diligent in using the helps of Thy grace for our eternal salvation.

O Lord, righteousness belongeth unto Thee, and unto us only confusion of face. But unto Thee, O Lord our God, belong also mercies and forgivenesses, though we have rebelled against Thee. For Thou, Lord, art good, and ready to forgive, and plenteous in mercy unto all them that call upon Thee. Look upon us, therefore, O righteous and holy Father, with an eye of pity and compassion, as we now humble ourselves, with sincere confession, before the throne

of Thy heavenly grace, and, for the sake of Thy Son Jesus Christ, speak pardon and peace to our souls. Let Thy mercy be upon us, O Lord, according as we hope in Thee. And with the full pardon of our past sins be pleased also to quicken us, we beseech Thee, in the way of righteousness, and uphold us with Thy free Spirit; that we may henceforth walk worthy of the vocation wherewith we are called, and ever hereafter serve and please Thee in newness of life, to the honour and glory of Thy holy name; through Jesus Christ our Lord.
Amen.

3.

We, poor sinners, confess before Thee, our Lord God and Creator, that we have grievously sinned in thought, in word, and in deed, neglecting the good and doing the evil, as Thou the searcher of hearts well knowest, and as we cannot enough deplore. We have broken the vows made unto Thee in our baptism, wherein we were made members of the body of Thy Son; we have not held fast the hope of His coming, neither have we purified ourselves as He is pure; we have not worthily praised Thee for Thy goodness, nor rendered unto Thee the glory due unto Thy name.

O merciful God, pardon these our transgressions for the sake of our Lord Jesus Christ, our only Mediator with Thee. As we from the heart forgive them that have sinned against us, do Thou show the like mercy unto us, and to all penitent sinners, and of Thy pity lead and guide us all from the misery of sin unto eternal life; through Jesus Christ our Lord. Amen.

4.

Most merciful Father, we acknowledge and confess before Thee that we are miserable sinners, conceived in sin, and brought forth in iniquity. We have broken the commandments of Thy just, holy, and good law, doing what Thou hast forbidden, and leaving undone what Thou hast enjoined. We have grievously offended Thee, not only by outward transgressions, but still more by inward iniquities of the heart. Nor have we sinned only through ignorance and infirmity, but also presumptuously, against the light of Thy Word, the checks of our consciences, and the strivings of Thy Holy Spirit, so that we have no cloak for our sins.

But yet, O Lord, we draw near to the throne of grace, hoping in Thy mercy. We trust in the all-sufficiency of that one sacrifice which Thy beloved Son hath offered for us on the cross, and in the efficacy of that intercession which He ever liveth to make for us at Thy right hand; and we most humbly beseech Thee, for His sake, to grant us the full and free remission of all our sins. Amen.

Prayers for Pardon and Peace.

1.

Almighty God, the Father of our Lord Jesus Christ, who desirest not the death of a sinner, but rather that he may turn from his wickedness and live; have mercy upon all here present who repent and turn to Thee; grant unto them full remission and forgiveness; absolve them from all their sins, iniquities, and transgressions, and vouchsafe unto them Thy Holy Spirit. **Amen.**

2.

Almighty God, and most merciful Father, who delightest not in the death of a sinner, but rather that he be converted from his sin and live; give unto Thy servants a deep contrition for their sins, a perfect hatred, and a full remission of them; visit us with the joys of Thy salvation, and the sweet sense that Thine anger is turned away from us; grant unto us grace to fear and love Thee, power and will to serve Thee, and time and space to finish the work which Thou hast given us to do; that we, being sprinkled with the blood of the lamb of God, may be justified by Thy grace, sanctified by Thy Spirit, and saved by Thine infinite and eternal goodness; through Jesus Christ our Lord. **Amen.**

3.

O Thou gracious God and Father of our Lord Jesus Christ, have mercy upon Thy servants who bow before Thee; pardon and forgive us all our sins; give us the grace of true repentance, and a strict obedience to Thy holy Word; strengthen us in the inner man for all the parts and duties of holy living; preserve us evermore in the unity of Thy Church, in the integrity of the Christian faith, in the love of Thee and of our neighbour, in the hope of eternal life, and in Thy peace which passeth all understanding.

Be pleased also to shed abroad Thy love in our hearts by the Holy Ghost, and to seal unto us, by the same spirit of adoption, the full assurance of pardon and reconciliation with Thee. Comfort all who mourn in Zion, speak peace to the wounded and troubled spirit, and bind up the broken-hearted, that we and all Thy people may be filled with joy and peace in believing, and may abound in hope, through the power of the Holy Ghost. **Amen.**

4.

Grant, we beseech Thee, merciful Lord, to Thy faithful people pardon and peace, that they may be cleansed from all their sins and serve Thee with a quiet mind; through Jesus Christ our Lord.
Amen.

Prayer of Dedication.

Unto Thee, O Lord, do we give thanks, for that Thy name is near Thy wondrous works declare. We approach unto Thee in the name of Jesus Christ, our Saviour, who hath died for our sins and risen again for our justification. We dedicate ourselves unto Thy service, yielding unto Thee our wills and our desires, our faculties, and all our members, the life of our body, the thoughts of our heart, the aspirations of our spirit. Perfect, O Lord, we beseech Thee, this our offering: let the fire of Thy love consume in us all sinful desires of the flesh and of the mind; that we may henceforth continually abide with Christ our Lord, seeking those things which are above, where He sitteth at Thy right hand. For unto Thee belongeth all glory, even unto the Father, and unto the Son, and unto the Holy Ghost: as it was in the beginning, is now, and ever shall be, world without end. **Amen.**

Supplications.

1.

Give ear, O Lord, unto our prayer, and attend to the voice of our supplication.

Make us poor in spirit: that ours may be the kingdom of heaven.

Make us to mourn for sin: that we may be comforted by Thy grace.

Make us meek: that we may inherit the earth.

Make us to hunger and thirst after righteousness: that we may be filled therewith.

Make us merciful: that we may obtain mercy.

Make us pure in heart: that we may see Thee.

Make us peacemakers: that we may be called Thy children.

Make us willing to be persecuted for righteousness' sake: that our reward may be great in heaven.

O God, true and highest Life, by whom, through whom, and in whom, all things live, which live truly and blessedly; pity and help us, according as Thou knowest we need, in body and in soul, that casting off all that entangles us, we may serve and cleave to Thee alone, who knowest all things, and canst perform all things, and who livest for evermore. **Amen.**

2.

Take from us that carnal mind which is death, and increase in us that spiritual mind which is life and peace.

Give us earnestness, strength of purpose, simplicity of faith, warmth of love.

Make us kindly in thought; gentle in word; generous in deed.

Teach us that it is better to give than to receive; better to forget ourselves than to put ourselves forward; better to minister than to be ministered unto; better to be last than to be first.

Preserve and keep us in the constant sense of our membership of Christ; in the unfailing thought that we are His soldiers and servants; in the love of our Father's house; and in the hope of our eternal home.

May we live by faith in Christ; may we increase in the joy of conscious union with Him; may we become more and more like Him, till we see Him as He is, and be changed into His perfect likeness.

Amen.

3.

Take from us all impurity of thought or desire; all envy, pride, hypocrisy; all falsehood and deceit; all covetousness, vainglory, and indolence; all malice and anger; everything that is contrary to Thy will, O most holy Lord.

Enlighten our understandings, that we may know the greatness of Thy love in Christ, the mysteries of Thy kingdom, and the riches of Thine eternal glory.

Teach us what Thou wouldst have us to do, and

uphold us by Thy mighty power, that every work of ours may begin always from Thee, and in Thee be happily ended. **Amen.**

4.

Hear, O Lord, our humble supplications.

Give us so to know Christ and His life, that the same mind which was in Him may be in us; that we may be in the world as He was in the world.

Give us so to know Christ and His death, that we may not glory save in His cross; whereby the world is crucified unto us, and we unto the world.

Give us so to know Christ and the power of His resurrection, that like as He was raised from the dead by the glory of the Father, we also may walk in newness of life.

Give us so to know Christ and His ascension, that our conversation may be in heaven; and that we may seek those things that are above, where He sitteth at Thy right hand.

Give us so to know Christ and His second coming, that our lamps may be burning and our loins girt, and we ourselves as servants waiting for their master.

Give us so to know Christ as Judge of quick and of dead, that we may give in our account with joy, and may be welcomed by Him to the kingdom of the Father. **Amen.**

5.

Hear, O Lord, our humble supplications.

Deliver us, we pray Thee, from ignorance and error, from prejudice and passion, from pride and self-confidence; and give us humble, teachable, and obedient hearts, that we may meekly receive whatsoever Thou hast taught us.

Make us ready to believe, where we cannot see; and willing to trust, where we cannot comprehend.

Let Thy Word be our light : Thine eye our guide : Thy love our law : and Thy presence our rest.

Enable us, as children of light and of the day, to renounce the hidden things of dishonesty, and to have no fellowship with the unfruitful works of darkness.

Grant that, walking in truth and uprightness, in purity and sincerity, before Thee, our fellowship may be with Thee the Father, and with Thy Son, Jesus Christ; and that, when the shadows of this life have passed away, we may enjoy the vision of Thy heavenly glory, and may ourselves shine forth, with the brightness of the sun, in Thy kingdom for ever and ever. **Amen.**

6.

O Thou Father of our Lord Jesus Christ, of whom the whole family in heaven and earth is named, we beseech Thee, according to the riches of Thy glory, to strengthen us with might by Thy Spirit in the inner man, that Christ may dwell in our hearts by faith; so that, being rooted and grounded in love, we may be able to comprehend with all saints what is the breadth, and length, and depth, and height, and to know the love of Christ, which passeth knowledge. **Amen.**

7.

O God, everlasting and Almighty, whose grace hath appeared, bringing salvation to all men; teach us to deny ungodliness and worldly lusts, and to live soberly, righteously, and godly in this present world; looking for that blessed hope, even the glorious appearing of our great God and Saviour Jesus Christ; who gave Himself for us, that He might redeem us from all iniquity, and purify unto Himself a peculiar people, zealous of good works. **Amen.**

8.

Almighty Father, who hast given Thine only Son to die for our sins, and to rise again for our justification, grant us so to put away the leaven of malice and wickedness, that we may alway serve Thee in pureness of living and truth; through the merits of the same, Thy Son, Jesus Christ our Lord.

Amen.

Intercessions.

1.

A Prayer for all conditions of men.

O God, the Creator and Preserver of all mankind, we humbly beseech Thee for all sorts and conditions of men, that Thou wouldst be pleased to make Thy ways known unto them, Thy saving health unto all nations. More especially we pray for the good estate of the Catholic Church; that it may be so guided and governed by Thy good Spirit, that all who profess and call themselves Christians may be led into the way of truth, and hold the faith in unity of spirit, in the bond of peace, and in righteousness of life. Finally, we commend to Thy fatherly goodness all those who are anyways afflicted or distressed in mind, body, or estate [especially those for whom our prayers are desired]; that it may please Thee to comfort and relieve them according to their several necessities, giving them patience under their sufferings, and a happy issue out of all their afflictions; and this we beg for Jesus Christ His sake. **Amen.**

2.

Short Form of Intercession, specially for use when there is a celebration of the Holy Communion.

We remember before Thee Thy Church militant here upon earth.

We pray Thee for all ministers of the Catholic Church, and for all baptized people.

We pray Thee to look down in mercy upon Thy desolate heritage, upon Thy scattered and divided people; heal the schisms of the Churches; put away all heresies from among them; bring back all who have wandered; cleanse Thy sanctuary from all defilement of superstition, will-worship, and infidelity; and grant unto Thy Church unity and peace.

We commend unto Thee the congregation here present, whose faith and piety do Thou accept and increase.

We pray Thee for the children of Christian parents, that they may be brought up in the nurture and admonition of the Lord. **Amen.**

We pray Thee for all kings, princes, and governors, and for all the people; especially for Thy servant Queen Victoria, for her whole council, and for all the people of her realm.

We pray Thee that Thou wilt give peace in our days.

We pray Thee for favourable weather, and that Thou wilt give unto us the fruits of the earth in due season. **Amen.**

We pray Thee for all Jews, Turks, infidels, and heretics, that Thou wilt turn their hearts. **Amen.**

We beseech Thee for all who are in trouble, sorrow, need, sickness, or any other adversity.

We commend unto Thee all departing this life; and we beseech Thee to receive them to Thy rest.
Amen.

We remember before Thee all those departed in the faith; the holy apostles and prophets, the evangelists and pastors; the blessed martyrs and confessors; and all Thy saints who have gone before.
Amen.

Hasten, O God, the time when Thou shalt send from Thy right hand Him whom Thou wilt send; at whose appearing the saints departed shall be raised, and we, which are alive, shall be caught up to meet Him, and so shall ever be with the Lord. Under the veil of earthly things we have now communion with Him; but with unveiled face we shall then behold Him, made like unto Him in His glory; and by Him we, with all Thy Church, holy and unspotted, shall be presented with exceeding joy before the presence of Thy glory. Hear us, O heavenly Father, for His sake, to whom, with Thee and the Holy Ghost, one living and true God, be glory for ever and ever. *Amen.*

3.

O God, in mercy remember Thine inheritance, and forget not the congregation of the poor for ever. Thou art our Redeemer and the lifter up of our head, and under the shadow of Thy wings shall we find our shelter and our rest.

Have mercy upon us, O God, and hide not Thyself from our petitions.

Preserve, O God, the Catholic Church in holiness and truth, in unity and peace. May she ever advance the honour of her Lord, for ever represent His sacrifice, glorify His Person, and advance His religion, that being accepted of Thee, and filled with His spirit, she may partake of His glory.

Have mercy upon us, O God, and hide not Thyself from our petitions.

Give the spirit of justice and righteousness to all Christian kings and governors; grant that their people may obey them, and that they may obey Thee. Especially do we pray for our Sovereign Lady the Queen, that she may reign in peace and in true religion, a partaker of Thy blessing here and of Thy kingdom of glory hereafter, through Jesus Christ our Lord.

Have mercy upon us, O God, and hide not Thyself from our petitions.

Give to Thy servants the clergy the spirit of patience and humility, of holiness and diligence, of prudence and courage, to declare Thy will by a pure life and wise words, that they may minister to the good of souls, and find the reward of the Master's approval at His coming.

Have mercy upon us, O God, and hide not Thyself from our petitions.

Give to our relatives and friends pardon of sin and the support of Thy grace, comfort in their sorrows, strength in their temptations, and the guidance of Thy good Spirit; that doing Thy will and rejoicing in Thy mercies here, they may partake of Thy glories hereafter.

Have mercy upon us, O God, and hide not Thyself from our petitions.

Give protection to all widows and orphans, patience and submission to the sick, consolation to the afflicted, that they may be rewarded by Thy comforts for the days wherein they have suffered adversity.

Have mercy upon us, O God, and hide not Thyself from our petitions.

Be Thou a star and a guide to them that travel by land or sea; the strength of them that toil in mines; give cheerfulness to sad hearts, and maintenance to the poor; be a defence to the oppressed, and bring to an end the miseries of all mankind.

Have mercy upon us, O God, and hide not Thyself from our petitions.

Give unto our enemies Thy forgiveness, charity to us, and love to Thee. Bring all sinners to repentance, and all Thy saints to perfect love and holiness; bring all unbelievers to the knowledge of the Lord Jesus, and to all the benefits of His passion; to the glory of His name.

Have mercy upon us, O God, and hide not Thyself from our petitions.

Give to all merchants faithfulness and truth; to the husbandman health and fair seasons, and reward his toil with the dew of heaven and the blessings of the earth. Give to all workmen diligence in their callings, and a blessing on their labours; give to the old a ripe religion, and desires after heaven; give to the young an early piety; give to all families Thy protection; and give to us all pardon, and holiness, and life eternal.

Have mercy upon us, O God, and hide not Thyself from our petitions.

4.

O Almighty and Eternal God, who in Christ hast revealed Thy glory to all nations, preserve, we beseech Thee, the works of Thine own mercy, that Thy Church which is spread over the whole world may persevere by steadfast faith in the confession of Thy name; through Jesus Christ our Lord.

O Almighty and Eternal God, by whose Spirit the whole body of the Church is governed and sanctified, receive our supplications for all estates of men, that by the gift of Thy grace every member of the same may faithfully serve Thee; through Christ our Lord.

O Almighty and Eternal God, in whose hand are the power of all and the rights of all kingdoms; graciously behold the empire of Christendom, that the nations which trust in their own fierceness may be restrained by the right hand of Thy power; through Jesus Christ our Lord.

O Almighty and Eternal God, the comfort of the sorrowful, the strength of those that travail in pain, let the prayers of such as call upon Thee in any manner of tribulation be heard by Thee, that all may rejoice that Thy mercy hath been present with them in their necessities; through Jesus Christ our Lord.

O Almighty and Eternal God, who desirest the salvation of all men, and willest not that any should perish, look mercifully on those souls that are deceived by the craft of the devil, that, laying aside all wickedness, malice, and heresy, the hearts of the erring may recover and return to the unity of Thy truth; through Jesus Christ our Lord.

O Almighty and Eternal God, who dost not reject from Thy mercy Thine ancient people the Jews, hear our prayers which we offer unto Thee on behalf of their blindness, that the veil may be taken from their hearts, and that they, acknowledging the light of Thy truth, which is the Christ, may be brought out of their darkness; through Jesus Christ our Lord.

O Almighty and Eternal God, who willest not the death of sinners, but always desirest their life, mercifully accept our prayers, and deliver the heathen from the worship of their idols, and, to the praise and glory of Thy name, bring them home to the flock of Thy holy Church; through Jesus Christ our Lord. Amen.

5.

O Lord God, our Father in heaven, we beseech Thee to visit Thy Church universal with the joy of Thy salvation. Endow her plenteously with spiritual gifts: preserve her also in truth and peace, in unity and safety, amidst all troubles, and against all temptations and enemies; that she, offering to Thee the never-ceasing sacrifice of praise and thanksgiving, may advance the honour of her Lord, and be filled with His Spirit, and partake of His glory.

Enrich with the graces of Thy Spirit those whom Thou hast set apart to minister in holy things; that they may serve Thee with clean hands and pure hearts; that they may be guides to the blind, and comforters to the weary and heavy-laden; that they may strengthen the weak and confirm the strong; that they may boldly rebuke sin, and patiently suffer for the truth.

O Thou Lord of the harvest, send forth, we pray Thee, labourers fitted to do the work of Thy harvest. Let the Sun of righteousness give light to those who sit in darkness. Let Thy Gospel have free course and be glorified.

Regard with the favour which Thou bearest unto Thine anointed, her most sacred Majesty the Queen. May she rule in Thy fear, be guided and sanctified by Thy Spirit, and be defended by Thine almighty power. Bless also and long preserve Albert Edward Prince of Wales, the Princess of Wales, and all the members of the Royal House.

Endue with grace, wisdom, and understanding the ministers of state [the members of both Houses of Parliament], and all governors, judges, and magistrates [especially the magistrates of this town]; that in their several offices they may advance Thy glory and the public good; and may the whole body of the people be distinguished by that righteousness which exalteth a nation.

O Thou helper of the helpless, our refuge in the time of trouble, be pleased to hear the cry of Thy persecuted and afflicted people. Speak peace to troubled consciences; send consolation to them that are in sorrow; instruct the ignorant, reclaim the erring, and supply the wants of the destitute. We beseech Thee to heal the sick, to ease the pains of the suffering, and to draw nigh in mercy to the dying [especially to any such known to ourselves, whom we name in our hearts before Thee], giving them faith in Thee, through Christ our Lord, in whom whoso believeth shall never die.

Be pleased, O Lord, to remember our kindred, friends, and benefactors; rewarding them with blessings, sanctifying them with Thy grace, and bringing them to Thine everlasting kingdom.

Almighty God, with whom do live the spirits of them that depart hence in the Lord, and with whom the souls of the faithful, after they are delivered from the burden of the flesh, are in joy and felicity; we give Thee thanks for all Thy servants departed this life in the true faith of Thy name; humbly entreating Thee to guide and sanctify us by Thy Spirit, that we also, and all Thy people, in due time, may be gathered into Thy Church triumphant, and reign with Christ our Lord in His eternal kingdom.

These things we ask, O heavenly Father, in patient confidence and joyful hope, being assured that we ask them according to Thy will, that the voice of Thy Church is heard by Thee, that the intercessions of the Holy Ghost are known unto Thee, and that the mediation of Thy well-beloved Son, our Lord and Saviour, doth prevail with Thee.

Wherefore, we glorify Thy name, we fall down before Thy throne, we worship and adore Thy glorious majesty; evermore praising Thee, and saying, Salvation be unto our God which sitteth upon the throne, and unto the Lamb for ever. Blessing, and glory, and wisdom, and thanksgiving, and honour, and power, and might, be unto our God for ever and ever. **Amen.**

6.

Prayer for the whole state of Christ's Church Militant here in Earth.

Almighty and ever-living God, who by Thy holy apostle hast taught us to make prayers and supplications, and to give thanks, for all men, we humbly beseech Thee most mercifully to receive these our prayers, which we offer unto Thy divine majesty; beseeching Thee to inspire continually the universal Church with the spirit of truth, unity, and concord. And grant that all they that do confess Thy holy name may agree in the Truth of Thy holy Word, and live in unity and godly love.

We beseech Thee also to save and defend all Christian kings, princes, and governors; and specially Thy servant Victoria, our Queen; that under her we may be godly and quietly governed. And grant unto her whole Council, and to all that are put in authority under her, that they may truly and impartially minister justice, to the punishment of wickedness and vice, and to the maintenance of Thy true religion and virtue.

Give grace, O heavenly Father, to all pastors and

ministers, that they may both by their life and doctrine set forth Thy true and lively Word, and rightly and duly administer Thy holy sacraments: and to all Thy people give Thy heavenly grace; and especially to this congregation here present, that, with meek heart and due reverence, they may hear and receive Thy holy Word, truly serving Thee in holiness and righteousness all the days of their life.

And we most humbly beseech Thee of Thy goodness, O Lord, to comfort and succour all them who in this transitory life are in trouble, sorrow, need, sickness, or any other adversity. And we also bless Thy holy name for all Thy servants departed this life in Thy faith and fear; beseeching Thee to give us grace so to follow their good examples, that with them we may be partakers of Thy heavenly kingdom. Grant this, O Father, for Jesus Christ's sake, our only Mediator and Advocate. Amen.

Thanksgivings.

1.

WE thank Thee for all the bounties of Thy providence; for health and strength, for food and raiment; for help and succour in times of need, for pity and consolation in times of sorrow; and for all the kindness Thou hast shown us from the beginning of our days until now. But above all, we thank Thee for Thine infinite love to us, miserable sinners; that Thou hast given Thy Son to be the propitiation for our sins; that Thou hast sent down Thy Holy

Spirit to sanctify our corrupt natures; that Thou dost favour us with the means of grace, and comfort us with the hope of glory.

Help us, we beseech Thee, to acknowledge Thy goodness, in all time to come, by trusting entirely in Thee, by contentment with the portion Thou hast given us, by charity to the poor and needy, by zeal for Thy truth, and by a cheerful obedience to Thy commandments. **Amen.**

2.

We render thanks unto Thy name, O God, most high; for Thou hast created us in Thine own image; Thou hast given us souls to know and love Thee; Thou hast made us but a little lower than the angels; Thou hast supplied all our wants; Thou hast loaded us with Thy benefits; Thou hast caused our cup to run over.

We have sinned against Thee, but Thou hast spared us; we have wandered from Thee, but Thou hast sought us; we were lost, but Thou hast saved us. O God our Saviour, Thou hast broken our chains, that we might be free; Thou hast healed our diseased souls, that we might not perish: Thou hast enriched us who were poor with the treasures of Thy salvation; Thou hast made us who had nothing to inherit all things; and even now, all things are ours. Therefore, with one heart and with one voice, we laud and magnify Thy glorious name; and, with Thy saints on earth and in heaven, we ascribe blessing, and honour, and glory, and power, unto Him that sitteth upon the throne, and unto the Lamb, for ever and for ever. **Amen.**

Prayers for Illumination.

1.

O God, whose Word is quick and powerful, and sharper than any two-edged sword, grant unto us who are here before Thee that we may receive Thy truth into our hearts, in faith and love. By it may we be taught and guided, upheld and comforted; that we be no longer children in understanding, but grow to the stature of perfect men in Christ, and be prepared to every good word and work, to the honour of Thy name; through Jesus Christ our Lord.
Amen.

2.

O God, who hast promised that in the last days the mountain of the Lord's house shall be exalted above the hills, and all nations shall flow unto it; send forth Thy light and Thy truth now unto Thy servants; leading them in the paths of Thine ordinances, and in the ways of Thy commandments; that we and Thy whole Church, perfect in every member, complete in holiness and instructed in righteousness, may be presented before Thee without spot or blemish, in the day of the appearing and kingdom of the Lord Jesus. *Amen.*

3.

Blessed Lord, who hast caused all holy Scriptures to be written for our learning; grant that we may in such wise hear them, read, mark, learn, and inwardly digest them, that by patience and comfort of

Thy holy Word we may embrace and ever hold fast the blessed hope of everlasting life, which Thou hast given us in our Saviour Jesus Christ. **Amen.**

4.

Prevent us, O Lord, in all our doings, with Thy most gracious favour, and further us with Thy continual help; that in all our works begun, continued, and ended in Thee, we may glorify Thy holy name, and finally by Thy mercy obtain everlasting life; through Jesus Christ our Lord. **Amen.**

Prayers after Sermon.

1.

O God, who art the guide and shepherd of all faithful souls, grant unto us who have now tasted of Thy goodness, that the eyes of our spirit may never cease to see Thee, nor our ears to hear Thy voice; that so we, constantly remembering Thy love and goodness towards men, may with a pure heart and faithful mind give ourselves to serve and follow Thee; through Jesus Christ our Lord. **Amen.**

2.

O God, who hast caused the light of Thy Word clearly to shine among us, and hast plainly instructed us in the way of salvation, shine into our hearts, we beseech Thee, by Thy Holy Spirit, that we being filled with the knowledge of Thy will, and animated with the hope of Thy promises, may in all things adorn the doctrine of our Saviour, and walk worthy of God, who hath called us unto His kingdom and glory. **Amen.**

3.

Almighty God, who hast builded Thy Church upon the foundation of the apostles and prophets, Jesus Christ Himself being the chief corner-stone; grant that, being illuminated through the words of Thy prophets, and joined together in unity of spirit through the doctrine, precepts, and ministry of Thine apostles, we may grow unto a holy temple in the Lord, and may be builded together for Thy habitation, through the Spirit. **Amen.**

4.

O God our Father, we beseech Thee to accept our worship. Pardon its imperfections; and grant that henceforth, putting all our trust in Thy well-beloved Son, enlightened by His teaching, guided by His example, and sanctified by His Spirit, we may walk in newness of life, and so prepare for that blessed life which Thou hast promised to Thy children in heaven.

Hear us, O merciful Father, in these our supplications, for the sake of Thy dear Son Jesus Christ, our Lord; to whom, with Thee and the Holy Ghost, be all honour and glory, world without end. **Amen.**

5.

O Lord our God, who hast shown great mercy to us Thy sinful and unworthy servants, upon whom Thy holy name is called, put us not to shame for our hope in Thee; but grant us, Lord, all these our petitions, and count us worthy to love and fear Thee with all our hearts, and to do in all things Thy most holy will. For Thou, O God, art good, and lovest all mankind. And to Thee we ascribe all glory, to the Father, and to the Son, and to the Holy Ghost, now and for evermore. **Amen.**

6.

O heavenly Father, that which is good and profitable do Thou supply unto us. Give us the peace that cometh from above, and also peace in this world. Grant that we may spend the remainder of this day in Thy fear; and may Thy goodness and mercy follow us all our days, and may we dwell in Thy house for ever. **Amen.**

7.

O God, who hast revealed to us the light of Thy Gospel, and called us into the fellowship of Thy Son Jesus Christ, bless to us Thy Word which we have heard this day; and grant that we may put away the works of darkness, and may walk in purity, uprightness, and sincerity; that we may have fellowship with Thee, for Thou art light, and with Thee there is no darkness at all; that, when the shadows of this mortal life are passed away, we may behold the King in His beauty, and be made partakers of

His everlasting glory; through the same Jesus Christ our Lord. **Amen.**

8.

Be present, O Lord, to our prayers, and protect us by day and by night; keep us watchful for the appearing of Thy beloved Son; and grant that in all the changes of this world, we may ever be strengthened by Thine unchangeableness; through Jesus Christ our Lord, to whom, with Thee and the Holy Ghost, be the glory, as it was in the beginning, is now, and ever shall be, world without end. **Amen.**

9.

Almighty God, who hast given us grace at this time with one accord to make our common supplications unto Thee, and dost promise that when two or three are gathered together in Thy name Thou wilt grant their requests; fulfil now, O Lord, the desires and petitions of Thy servants, as may be most expedient for them; granting us in this world knowledge of Thy truth, and in the world to come life everlasting. **Amen.**

Ascriptions of Glory.

1.

NOW unto Him that is able to do exceeding abundantly above all that we ask or think, according to the power that worketh in us; unto Him be glory in the Church by Christ Jesus, throughout all ages, world without end. **Amen.**

2.

Now unto Him that is able to keep us from falling, and to present us faultless before the presence of His glory with exceeding joy; to the only wise God our Saviour, be glory and majesty, dominion and power, both now and ever. **Amen.**

3.

Unto Him that loved us, and washed us from our sins in His own blood, and hath made us kings and priests unto God, His Father; to Him be glory and dominion for ever and ever. **Amen.**

4.

Now unto the blessed and only Potentate, the King of kings and Lord of lords; who only hath immortality, dwelling in the light which no man can approach unto; whom no man hath seen or can see: to Him be honour and power everlasting. **Amen.**

5.

Now unto the God of all grace, who hath called us unto His eternal glory by Christ Jesus, be glory and dominion for ever and ever. **Amen.**

6.

And now to the Father, Son, and Holy Ghost, three Persons and one God, be ascribed by us, and by the whole Church, as is most due, the kingdom, the power, and the glory, for ever and ever.

Amen.

7.

Unto the Father, and unto the Son, and unto the Holy Ghost, be ascribed in the Church all honour and glory, might, majesty, dominion, and blessing, now, henceforth, and for ever. *Amen.*

Milton Keynes UK
Ingram Content Group UK Ltd.
UKHW022023170823
427026UK00007B/354